M000238644

MAKING CONNECTIONS

TERRY G. CARTER & PREBEN VANG

MAKING CONNECTIONS

Finding Your Place in God's Story

WEAVER BOOK
COMPANY
WOOSTER, OHIO

Making Connections: Finding Your Place in God's Story

© 2015 by Terry G. Carter & Preben Vang

Published by
Weaver Book Company
1190 Summerset Dr.
Wooster, OH 44691
Visit us at weaverbookcompany.com

All rights reserved. No part of this book may be reproduced, stored in a retrieval system, or transmitted in any form or by any means—electronic, mechanical, photocopy, recording or otherwise—without written permission of the publisher, except for brief quotations in printed reviews.

All Scripture quotations, unless otherwise indicated, are from the Holy Bible, English Standard Version (ESV), copyright © 2001 by Crossway, a publishing ministry of Good News Publishers. Used by permission. All rights reserved.

All sidebars and illustrations, including maps and charts, are copyright © by B & H Publishing Group. Used by permission. Chart "Abrahamic Covenant vs. Mosaic Covenant" prepared by J. Daniel Hays. Used by permission.

Cover design: Frank Gutbrod
Editorial, design, and production:
　　　{ In a Word } www.inawordbooks.com
　　　/edited by Rebekah Matt/
ISBN: 978-1-941337-07-3

15 16 17 18 19/ 5 4 3 2 1
Printed in the United States of America

CONTENTS

PREFACE

Terry G. Carter

I am a great fan of the timeless Arthur Conan Doyle character, Sherlock Holmes. Holmes possesses marvelous gifts of deduction, which he uses to interpret apparently random clues. With some help from his insightful sidekick, Dr. John Watson, he solves seemingly impossible cases. To a novice sleuth, these apparently unconnected pieces of information paint a confused picture. Many people struggle with putting pieces together to make one complete story. We need a Sherlock Holmes to help us.

In our churches we often expect members to take all the pieces of the larger story of redemption and put them all together. Preachers and teachers often preach series or individual sermons on biblical books and passages in a fashion that may seem random to the congregant. Members gain solid information about the parts of the story that are beneficial. Unfortunately, we have developed a church membership that possesses information about things found in the biblical story but really does not see the whole story or understand its meaning. They grasp that the Bible consists of sixty-six books all placed together to make up one book, but fail to perceive that all these books combined tell one overarching story of redemption. The metanarrative of the Bible never really gets proper attention. But it should!

One reason is the importance of context. Context stands as one of the most critical issues in truly understanding anything. On a trip with several friends years ago, three of us overheard another friend during a phone conversation. He mentioned words like "bucket" and "pulling out." This led to a humorous interaction as we tried to interpret his meaning with only one side of the conversation. We needed context. When we hear only one side of a conversation, we often miss the heart of the message. We need the whole story. Church members hear a sermon about David and gain valuable information about the man and his heart, but how much more would the story mean with an understanding of where David fits into the whole narrative?

In teaching the Bible to incoming freshmen, Dr. Vang and I discovered that even after hearing numerous church sermons and attending many Sunday school and Bible study lessons, students lacked the metanarrative knowledge. They struggled to put it all together or even to place a piece of the story in its proper chronological and theological position.

So we asked ourselves, what needs to happen? Students, church members, laypeople, and even church leaders benefit from a walk-through the story of the Bible. As an answer to this need, we developed and wrote a textbook clearly laying out the metanarrative biblical story with its redemptive focus. This book, *Telling God's Story: The Biblical Narrative from Beginning to End,* was first published by Broadman & Holman in 2006 and then followed by a revision with maps, pictures, charts, and graphics in 2013. The text has been used in university classrooms and churches for eight years. But since the story is so large, we discovered that students could benefit from a workbook with exercises designed to get them into the text and the story and prepare them for class discussions. The current publication is the result of that discovery. *Making Connections* refers to *Telling God's Story* and works well as a companion to the book. However, it also serves well as a guide for any biblical metanarrative class taught by a teacher using the textbook and/or the Bible. A motivated individual Bible student might also find the workbook a helpful guide to the story.

The workbook breaks the narrative down into episodes and acts (as does *Telling God's Story*) signifying God's dramatic story unfolding in parts. Each act of the drama offers students questions from three perspectives, allowing them to think deeply about what God is saying and doing in the story. Students encounter questions to help guide them through the reading of the story, questions to aid in discovering the meaning of the story, and finally, questions designed to help them find their own place in God's redemptive story. Each act is introduced and concluded with pieces of the biblical story, allowing easy transition from one section to the next. Completion of an act in the workbook prepares students for discussion and a deeper understanding of key biblical truths revealed as the story unfolds.

Background information and context provide key aids to deeper understanding of biblical truth. *Telling God's Story* includes a long overview of the redemptive story and a biblical backgrounds section. A shorter background section and a story summary are included in *Making Connections* as part of the introduction. The information contained in these sections offers valuable information to the reader for clearer understanding and interpretation of the biblical story.

So prepare yourself for a journey through the Bible focused on the big picture of how God created everything and then prepared and carried out his plan to redeem all human beings. This trek offers life-changing truths, and if you approach it with an open mind and heart, you will discover its power. One of the many benefits of this journey is to allow yourself (perhaps for the first time) to see the big picture and understand how all the parts and actors of the story fit and matter. It's God's story as unveiled in the Bible, which has for centuries changed people eternally and continues to do so. Enjoy the trip!

BACKGROUND TO THE BIBLE STORY

Preben Vang

TESTAMENTS AND COVENANTS

The Bible consists of two testaments—the Old and the New. The New does not replace the Old; rather, together they reveal the full story of the covenantal relationship between God and his people. The Old Testament describes how and when God first made these covenants with a chosen people. The New Testament explains and describes how God fulfilled these in a *new* covenant with people from all places and of all races. Since God is not discontinuous, the two testaments are not disjointed. The new covenant, which is the covenant established through Jesus Christ, results from the previous promises God gave to Abraham and David.

TWO MAJOR DIVISIONS IN SCRIPTURE	
Old Testament	New Testament
First or Early Covenants	Last Covenant
Promises	Fulfillment
39 books	27 books

ONE BIG STORY—66 BOOKS
THE STORY OF GOD'S PURPOSE FOR HIS CREATION

The connection between the two sections of the Bible might be described in this way: God constituted his special relationship with humankind in the creation event itself. To enable an expression of reciprocal love, humans were given a free will—and they chose to reject God. What God created, humankind devastated!

God then created a series of covenants. The first was the Abrahamic covenant. God promised Abraham that he, as the father of those who have faith in God, would become a great people. This was an *unconditional* promise from God. Still, although God continued to give expressions of his love (most prominently the Exodus event), people persisted in their rejection of God. To give guidance to his people, God used Moses as the mediator of a legal covenant that based the relationship between God and humans on a *conditional* statement of Law. As long as the people kept the Law, God's presence and power would be present.

Although people broke the Mosaic covenant, they could not break the covenant promised to Abraham. The Abrahamic covenant came close to its fulfillment during the reign of David. David received the promise that an eternal dynasty would be established in his lineage—a promise that found its fulfillment in the new covenant.

Ezekiel and Jeremiah prophesied concerning this new covenant that it was to be a covenant of the Spirit. Isaiah foresaw that God instituted a new covenant through his Suffering Servant who was to pay with his life to make this possible. After the death, resurrection, and ascension of his Son, God sent his Holy Spirit to convince humans from within about God's desire for relationship. Given to people of faith, this Spirit of the new covenant realizes the promise of the old covenants given to Abraham and David.

THE BIBLE AND ITS BOOKS

Beyond the two major divisions of the Bible, each of the testaments contains different sections. Broadly speaking, they follow a historical line from creation to the return from the exile and the promise of the new covenant.

Outside of the sixty-six canonical books, the early church made use of another set of writings relating to the Old Testament. These are called the Apocrypha and were considered helpful for private study and edification. These are included in Catholic translations, but not in most Protestant translations.

THE DIVISIONS OF THE BOOKS IN THE CHRISTIAN OLD TESTAMENT				
PENTATEUCH (MOSTLY LAW MATERIAL)	HISTORICAL BOOKS	POETRY AND WISDOM	PROPHETIC BOOKS	
			MAJOR PROPHETS	MINOR PROPHETS
Genesis	Joshua	Job	Isaiah	Hosea
Exodus	Judges	Psalms	Jeremiah	Joel
Leviticus	Ruth	Proverbs	Lamentations	Amos
Numbers	1 & 2 Samuel	Ecclesiastes	Ezekiel	Obadiah
Deuteronomy	1 & 2 Kings	Song of Solomon	Daniel	Jonah
	1 & 2 Chronicles			Micah
	Ezra			Nahum
	Nehemiah			Habakkuk
	Esther			Zephaniah
				Haggai
				Zechariah
				Malachi

APOCRYPHA		
1 Esdras	Ecclesiasticus	Prayer of Manasseh
2 Esdras	Baruch	1 Maccabees
Tobit	Letter of Jeremiah	2 Maccabees
Judith	Song of the Three	Psalm 151
Additions to Esther	Susanna	
Wisdom of Solomon	Bel and the Dragon	

Although the material of the New Testament differs vastly from that of the Old Testament, there is still a clear pattern to its order. Four types of literature give structure to the arrangement. The Gospels are a kind of historical/theological biography of Jesus in which biographical elements become the launching pad for theological truth. Following the Gospels, Acts is a historical description of the spread of the early church and its message. The book of Acts recounts how the presence of God's Spirit (beginning with Acts 2) empowered the early disciples to accomplish the commission given them by Jesus (Acts 1:8).

A series of letters follows Acts. Paul wrote the first thirteen of these, all of which are named according to their recipients and deal with problems and issues specific to those churches or people. The exception is the letter to the Romans, which reads more like a theological treatise than do his other letters.

The letters that follow Paul's are called the General Letters, or the Catholic Letters. Rather than addressing the issues of specific churches, these letters predominantly give teaching on theological issues facing the early church in general. Except for Hebrews, the General Letters receive their name from the author who wrote them. The New Testament concludes with the book of Revelation. Written during times of persecution, its apocalyptic genre resembles similar literature of the time. Revelation gives hope and promise to suffering Christians. God will ultimately be victorious over the forces of evil.

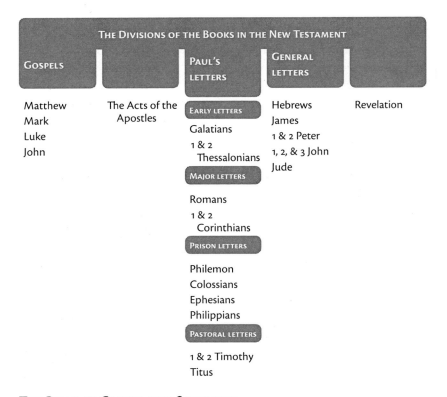

THE DIVISIONS OF THE BOOKS IN THE NEW TESTAMENT			
GOSPELS		PAUL'S LETTERS	GENERAL LETTERS

Matthew	The Acts of the	**EARLY LETTERS**	Hebrews	Revelation
Mark	Apostles	Galatians	James	
Luke		1 & 2	1 & 2 Peter	
John		Thessalonians	1, 2, & 3 John	
		MAJOR LETTERS	Jude	
		Romans		
		1 & 2		
		Corinthians		
		PRISON LETTERS		
		Philemon		
		Colossians		
		Ephesians		
		Philippians		
		PASTORAL LETTERS		
		1 & 2 Timothy		
		Titus		

THE BIBLE AS CANON AND SCRIPTURE

Although the Bible is a book filled with accounts of God's dealings with people, it is not open-ended. As Scripture, the Bible gives God's final, authoritative, and revelatory word about himself and his creation. That the Bible is a revelation from God means that it is both willed and informed by God.

We call the process of protecting God's Word from fraudulent texts and false theology *canonization*. The word *canon* comes from a Greek word that means "rule or standard." The word was used to denote that the 66 books chosen were authoritative as a guide/rule for belief and behavior.

Although the road to canonization went through rugged terrain, the identification of the Old Testament texts as sacred and inspired came about quite early. As early as 250 BC, the Hebrew texts of the Jewish Bible were translated into Greek and came to be called the Septuagint (LXX). The LXX quickly became Scripture for all Greek-speaking believers, including Paul and the early church.

In the early church the necessity of canonization flowed directly from the need to protect the church from false teachers. As early as Paul's missionary journeys, forgeries were circulated that falsely claimed the authority of the apostles (cf. Gal. 6:11). As the church spread rapidly, itinerant teachers and preachers of various backgrounds and insight became the messengers of the Christian gospel. Diversity flourished and, as the letters of the New Testament clearly show, guidance became mandatory.

Selecting and collecting the New Testament writings into what we now know as the canon was a slow process. As the reference in 2 Peter 3:15–16 shows, Paul's letters were recognized as inspired very early. The earliest reference to all four of the canonical Gospels included in the New Testament comes from a letter written by Clement, a famous bishop in Rome, writing early in the second century. Although the final demarcation of the New Testament writings from other edifying material did not come until the fourth century, the second-century church leaders had already ranked Paul's letters, the four Gospels, and Acts as canonical. The General Letters, especially Jude, 2 Peter, 2 and 3 John, and Revelation, were the latest to find general acceptance.

Three criteria were given for the selection of the twenty-seven books of the New Testament. First, it had to be written by an apostle or an eyewitness. Mark and Luke did not fulfill this criterion, but their close relationship with Peter and Paul, respectively, was considered sufficient. Second, it had to have been generally accepted either by a leading church or by the majority of the churches. Third, it had to have spiritual integrity and practical value. It had to be in accord with sound doctrine and bear the marks of divine inspiration.

READING THE BIBLE

Everyone who reads a text does so with a set of presuppositions. There is no such thing as a completely open mind. This also holds true when people read the Bible. If they choose to reject its content even before they begin, they miss its point and will not experience its transforming power. To be open-minded means to give the biblical text a chance to address people on its own terms.

THE BIBLE STORY: AN OVERVIEW

Preben Vang

The story of the Bible begins with God. In the beginning, God created the universe. God is not a part of the universe as a mere power but is a separate and independent Creator who willfully and deliberately created everything that exists. Being an expression of God's own beauty, love, and relational character, creation belongs to God. Everything in creation, therefore, from the smallest and seemingly most insignificant to the crowning work, the human being, finds its meaning and reason for existence in the relationship between the Creator and his creation.

To express his love, God decided to give to creation an expression of his own image—the human being. He created the human being as man and woman and gave them managerial power over the rest of creation. They were to live in a close and loving relationship with their Creator and conduct their lives as an expression of that relationship. Human beings, however, decided that they could live on their own without God. This decision destroyed the intimacy of their relationship with the Creator, and as this relationship deteriorated, the image of God faded, and humans lost the true quality of their humanity.

Outside God's presence human beings experienced the results of the destroyed fellowship with God. Blessing had been exchanged for curse. Envy, pain, and evil (even to the point of murder) became commonplace. Humans proved that the goodness and love that came from the presence of God were annihilated by their own desire to put themselves first. Sin, which in its essence is the rebellion of humans against God, had become the governing quality of humankind. Evil grew and covered the earth; God was forgotten.

The never-ending grace of God, however, would not let go of the crowning work of creation. Rather than withdrawing, God established a new covenantal relationship with humankind. A man named Abraham, who is now considered the Father of Faith (Luke 16:24; Rom. 4:16–5:2; Heb. 11:17) because of his unwavering trust in God, received a promise that his numerous descendants would be blessed. In fact, blessing would come to the whole earth through them. Because of this covenant promise given to Abraham, all the people of the earth would have the opportunity to experience the blessing of God's presence once again.

The promise to Abraham was a unilateral promise; that is, it was a promise from God with no condition placed on man. It was an expression of pure grace: God placed it solely upon himself to reestablish the relationship with the rebellious creatures he originally had created in his own image. This Abrahamic covenant thus became the basis for the salvation of human beings. Again and again, in spite of the repeated attempts by humans to destroy their relationship with the Creator, God remembered his covenant with Abraham and opened a door for humans to find a way back into his presence.

At first it looked as if God's promise was empty; Abraham was without children. But in Abraham's old age, God granted him the son of promise, Isaac, who in turn became the father of a son, Jacob. Jacob, whom God later renamed Israel, had twelve sons whose names would later give rise to the names of Israel's twelve tribes. God had created for himself a people called Israel. This people, also called the Hebrews, were to be recognized and characterized by their trust in the one true God, the Creator of heaven and earth.

Famine came upon the land, and the family of Jacob went to Egypt to find food. In Egypt the people of Israel increased in number; and as time passed, the Egyptian rulers, called pharaohs, worried that the Israelites would become too powerful. To counter this threat, the pharaohs enslaved the Israelites and killed their newborn baby boys. For approximately 400 years the faithful among the people cried to God for help in their misery. In these darkest of days, an Egyptian princess found an Israelite baby boy floating on the river in a basket woven by his mother who attempted to save his life. His name was Moses. The princess took him and raised him as an Egyptian prince. When he came of age, Moses realized his Hebrew heritage and left Egypt to live in the desert. Remembering his covenant with Abraham, God called Moses in the desert and charged him with the task of liberating his people from their bondage in Egypt. Moses at first refused, arguing that he did not even know the name of Israel's God. From out of a burning bush, God revealed himself to Moses as Yahweh, the I AM, the one who is always present with his people.

Moses returned to Egypt, imploring Pharaoh to let the Hebrews go, but Pharaoh would not listen. Plagues sent by God invaded the land, but Pharaoh still did not listen—not even when God gave his last warning. Yahweh promised to send the angel of death to visit every household in Egypt and kill the firstborn of all families unless Pharaoh released Israel from slavery and allowed them to leave Egypt to worship God in the desert.

To avoid death in the families of Israel, God told his people to make a meal in haste. They then took the blood of a lamb and smeared it on the door frames to let the angel of death know that he was to *pass over* their homes. God would save his people by the blood of the lamb.

After this final plague, Egypt let Israel go, even hurrying them along. Israel left and came to the sea of reeds.[*] By this time the Egyptians regretted

---

[*] The original Hebrew text says *Yam Suph*, which means "sea of reeds." The reference is probably not to the Red Sea as we normally think of that body of water.

their decision to release the slaves and sent out armies to take them back. The Hebrews were caught between the water and the Egyptian army. They were trapped; the only one way of escape was through the water—an impossible situation.

God kept his promise to Abraham, however, and opened the waters for them to cross to the other side. The Egyptians, close behind, drowned on the bottom of the sea as God closed the waters as soon as Israel passed through. God had rescued his people! He had created for them an *exodus*—a way out of slavery. They were now on their way to the land God had promised them, free to follow him and to live in his presence. He would guide them through the desert by a cloud during the day and a pillar of fire during the night.

A new situation had become a reality for Israel. Yahweh was in the midst of his people; the holy Creator God lived among humans. He dwelled among them in a tabernacle—a portable tent designed for worship, the celebration of God's presence.

How were people to live in this new situation? What guidelines should govern this new relationship? God called Moses to a mountaintop and gave him a set of rules consisting of Ten Commandments—Ten Commandments that became the foundation for a new bilateral covenant, called the Mosaic covenant. It was bilateral because demands were put on both parties in the relationship. Yahweh promised he would be their God, they would be his people, and he would dwell in their midst. They were to keep the Law expressed in the commandments. Beyond the Ten Commandments, other rules and regulations were written down to define how the Israelites should live and worship the God in their midst. As a legal covenant the Mosaic covenant required man's obedience to the Law as its central feature. This was different from the Abrahamic covenant, which had God's faithfulness to his promise as its central feature.

As usual, God kept his end of the agreement. He led the people to the edge of the land promised to Abraham—Canaan, but when they arrived, they were afraid to take possession of the land. This lack of trust in God sent them back into the desert to wander for forty years. Only after that faithless generation had died off did Yahweh again lead them to enter the land. After Moses' death Joshua became the leader of the people, and he led them to victory after victory until they took possession of the land God had promised them.

Following Joshua's death in the promised land, a series of judges became leaders of the people. People like Gideon, Deborah, and Samson led Israel's armies and passed judgment on the people. This is sometimes considered the dark age of Hebrew history. Not only did many of the people stop worshiping Yahweh, but several of the judges were active in worshiping idols. It was a dark day for the relationship between God and his people. But as before, God ended the misery of his people. The time of the judges came to an end when Israel chose to have a king like the other peoples.

During the reign of the second of these kings, King David, the promise from God approached its fulfillment for the nation of Israel. The Abrahamic covenant—with its promise of land, blessing, and peace—came close to a complete fulfillment during David's reign. David was Yahweh's answer to the destitution caused by the period of the judges. He was a man after God's own heart, a shepherd boy whose greatest desire was to please God. Under David the kingdom grew to hitherto unknown size and greatness. David made Jerusalem the capital of Israel and sought to build Yahweh a temple. This task, however, fell to his son, Solomon.

Nonetheless, God was pleased with David's desire to build a temple for Yahweh's presence among his people, and so he extended a covenant promise to David. God promised to make David's name great, grant an eternal place for his people, and establish a permanent dynasty in the Davidic line. This Davidic covenant, like the Abrahamic, was a unilateral covenant with no condition placed on humans for its fulfillment. It forms the basis for Israel's hope as later expressed by the prophets and most climactically underscored in the genealogies of Jesus.

Solomon, who followed his father David as king, became world renowned for his wisdom and incredible wealth. Out of this wealth he built Yahweh a temple in Jerusalem. Upon its completion, the Bible explains how God filled the temple with his presence. Solomon disobeyed God in other areas, however, and "did not have the heart of his father." Solomon's sin led to the split of the kingdom after his death. Ten tribes followed Jeroboam, a former general under Solomon who established the kingdom of Israel in the north; two tribes stayed with Rehoboam, Solomon's son, to establish the kingdom of Judah in the south. These two nations picked up where the judges left off and continued the destruction of their relationship with God. Even priests replaced the worship of Yahweh with the worship of Baal, a Canaanite god. The people seemed intent on breaking the Mosaic covenant.

During this time, the eighth century before Christ, prophets spoke out from both the northern and southern kingdoms, warning the people of the imminent judgment of God. The prophetic message proclaimed God's indictment on the people. God's people had violated the covenant by their idolatry, their social injustice, and their religious formalism. "You have broken the covenant," the prophets charged, "you must repent! If there is no repentance, judgment will come!" And judgment came! The Assyrians destroyed the Northern Kingdom of Israel in 721 BC; and Babylon destroyed Judah in 586 BC, forcing a large number of Hebrews into exile in Babylon. The people had broken their covenantal relationship with God, and they now had to rely solely on the hope of restoration, which had always been part of the prophetic message.

During the exile the focus of the people changed. Prophets like Ezekiel (similar to Jeremiah before him) looked forward to a time when God's law would no longer be written on tablets of stone but on human hearts—a time when God's Spirit would indwell every member of God's family to ensure an internal drawing toward God's word and will. God will establish a new covenant with his people, they proclaimed. Daniel, a devout young man from Judah, who counseled the king of Babylon during the exile, saw a vision of someone like a Son of Man who possessed authority and who was to create an everlasting kingdom. People from all nations and all languages would come to worship this Son of Man. It was a time of renewed hope.

The Mosaic covenant was shattered, but the prophets were looking back to the unilateral covenants given to Abraham and David. God would no longer limit his presence to the temple in Jerusalem. Ezekiel shared a vision in which God's throne was on wheels moving in every direction. In the days to come, God would move with his people as in the days of old—not just among them as with the tabernacle but within them through his Spirit. The glory that had left the temple would be manifested through the people of the Spirit.

When Persia conquered Babylon, the Persians allowed the people of Israel to return. After seventy years of exile, Zerubbabel led God's people back to the promised land to rebuild the temple. The restoration of the wall around Jerusalem and the reestablishment of the full worship of Yahweh came later under the leadership of Ezra and Nehemiah. These leaders of Israel made great efforts to bring Israel back to pre-exilic times. But it never happened! Yahweh did not return to fill the temple as he did under Solomon. The nation of Israel did not become truly independent. The Mosaic covenant had been broken, and it would not be restored. The Law no longer defined the covenant relationship between God and his people; it functioned simply as a rigorous guideline for living. The period after the exile, the so-called postexilic period, functioned as an interim period between the judgment of the exile and the promise of a new covenant restoration where God once again would be visible among his people. This new covenant, which prophets like Jeremiah, Joel, Ezekiel, and others had prophesied about, was to be a covenant of the Spirit.

The people had broken the bilateral Mosaic covenant, but God remembered his covenant with Abraham and David. In the fullness of time, some 400 years later, he sent his own Son in the form of a human to fulfill the promises of blessing to the world and eternal kingship on David's throne. The New Testament begins its story by placing this Son in the lineage of both David and Abraham.

An angel of God visited a priest named Zechariah while he was ministering in the temple and told him that his wife Elizabeth would give birth to a son who would be great in the eyes of God. The child, John, who became known as John the Baptist, served as the forerunner to the Messiah. His purpose was to announce to the people that the new covenant relationship God had promised was at hand. John the Baptist, in other words, served as a prophetic bridge between the old and new covenants.

God's angel, Gabriel, visited a young girl from Judah named Mary and told her that God's own Spirit would overshadow her and make her pregnant. The child to come should be called Jesus, which means Savior. He would become the long-awaited Messiah whom the prophets had looked for to save the world.

Jesus was born in simple circumstances and grew in wisdom, stature, and favor with God and man. At about thirty years of age, Jesus came to the desert where John the Baptist was preaching and baptizing, and he asked John to baptize him. As Jesus came up from the water, God initiated Jesus' ministry. The Holy Spirit descended upon him in the form of a dove, and God spoke the words: "You are my Son, whom I love; with you I am well pleased."

Everywhere he went, Jesus preached the message that God's kingdom had come near. For three years he walked and taught. His message was consistent in both word and deed. God's kingdom had come near. Some people were confused, however, because their expectations of the promised Messiah were so different from what they saw in Jesus. Even John the Baptist, who himself had looked forward to God's intervention, became confused and sent his disciples to ask Jesus if he was the one to come. Jesus sent these words back to John the Baptist: "Tell John what you have seen and heard. The blind receive sight, the lame walk, those with leprosy are cured, the deaf hear, the dead are raised, and the good news is preached to the poor."

The evidence was abundantly clear: God had come back to dwell among his people. His power overflowed, and the message of his presence was again proclaimed. The old prophetic indictment and warning that the people were destroying the covenant had been replaced by the proclamation that God was fulfilling his promise. The kingdom of God's saving rule was at hand. Jesus' message sounded just as clear as that of the prophets' of old: God wants his people for himself; there is no room for idolatry. "You must repent," Jesus said. God has no pleasure in religious formalism; what matters, said Jesus, is the heart. New covenant worshipers will worship in Spirit and in truth. God still hates social injustice. Jesus came to preach good news to the poor and to release the oppressed.

For the Jewish leaders, this message served as a radical indictment of their lifestyle, beliefs, and position. They plotted to kill Jesus and put an end to his growing group of disciples. It all came to a head during a week of Passover celebration. Jesus assembled his twelve closest disciples in an upper room to celebrate the Jewish Passover. Knowing what was about to happen, he told them of his imminent death. Gathered around the Passover table for a meal to remember how God saved them from slavery in Egypt, Jesus changed the symbolic content of the typical Jewish Passover meal and made it a celebration of the new covenant. Jesus took the bread and broke it, saying that it represented his body, which was about to be broken for many. He also poured the wine, saying that it represented his blood, which was about to be shed for the forgiveness of sins.

Later that evening he went to the garden of Gethsemane to pray. As he was praying, the Jewish leaders, escorted by a large number of soldiers and by Jesus' own disciple Judas, came out and took him captive. After an illegal trial before the Jewish Sanhedrin, Jesus stood before the Roman prefect Pontius Pilate for a Roman trial. Though he found him not guilty, Pilate still gave in to the pressure of the Jewish leaders who had stirred up the crowd against Jesus. Jesus was crucified on Friday—killed by the cruelest and most painful method of execution known to the Romans. That same day, when Jesus died, the pain of God, giving his own Son for the sins of humankind, became evident. The sun darkened and the temple's curtain, which separated the temple's holy area from its most holy area, tore from top to bottom. It was as if God had torn his clothes to express his own pain and suffering. At the same time, God had created open access into the place of his holy dwelling.

Jesus' death on the cross was not God's final word, however. By his sacrificial death, Jesus paid the price for the sins of humankind, opening the door for people again to enjoy the fellowship with God that sin had broken. Jesus died not just as a religious man but as the Son of God. God majestically and powerfully confirmed Jesus as his Son when Jesus rose from the dead on the third day. The resurrection vindicated Jesus' death as an act of God and verified his identity as the Son of God. As Paul would later say, without the resurrection faith in Jesus would have been meaningless. But, as it is, because he *did* rise, faith in Jesus means everything. It reestablishes a saving relationship between God and humans who put their trust in him.

During a forty-day period after his resurrection, Jesus appeared to his disciples to ensure them of his continued presence and to give them instructions for the future. He would ascend to heaven, he explained; and while he was there, the disciples were to continue to spread his message. Jesus commissioned his followers to make disciples of all nations by baptizing and teaching them everything that he had taught. The ascension is necessary, Jesus continued, because "unless I go back to my Father, the Holy Spirit will not come to you" (see John 16:7).

The Spirit came ten days after the ascension of Jesus. It happened on the day we now call Pentecost. The Spirit came with a power that enabled the ministry of Jesus to continue through his disciples. The Spirit brought the presence of God in a way that was unlimited by space and time. The first time the disciples preached, people from everywhere, who were assembled in Jerusalem for the Pentecost festival, heard the gospel and were moved to conversion—three thousand that first day. Before long the gospel spread far beyond Jerusalem, and the church became a powerful reality in the world.

This rapid growth of the church created strong opposition. One of the primary opponents was a young Pharisee named Paul. In spite of his young age, he had gained great prominence among the Jewish leaders. One day, on his way to Damascus to track down and persecute more Christians, a powerful vision of the resurrected Jesus stopped him. This encounter radically convinced Paul of the truth of the Christian message, and it led to his conversion and baptism. After a season, a prominent church member named Barnabas, who was ministering in the church in Antioch, called on Paul to come and help him there.

This ministry in Antioch gave impetus to the conviction that God wanted the gospel to be preached to all people everywhere. Paul and Barnabas now left the church in Antioch to take a journey into Asia Minor to spread the good news. Coming back from this first journey, Paul and Barnabas found that some Pharisees, although they had acknowledged that Jesus had come from God, were vehemently opposed to their ministry. These so-called Judaizers preached that people could only become Christians if they also would keep the Law of Moses. Paul and Barnabas were infuriated! To them the new covenant was a covenant of Spirit and faith, not of law and rituals. The so-called gospel of the Judaizers was no gospel at all.

To settle the matter, Paul and Barnabas went to talk to the leaders of the mother church in Jerusalem. In this meeting—after prayer, testimony, and conversation—it was determined that God did not require Gentiles (non-Jews) to become Jews before they could become Christians. By giving his Spirit to the Gentiles, God had already spoken on the matter, they concluded. Everyone who would trust in Jesus' death as atonement for human sin and who would recognize his resurrection as the manifestation of God's power over evil, belonged to God. The evidence that someone had become a Christian was the presence of God's Spirit, not the keeping of the Mosaic covenant. In this way the meeting in Jerusalem became the starting point for a powerful mission enterprise that would spread the gospel throughout the world.

Paul made at least three missionary journeys, starting churches everywhere from the province of Galatia through Asia Minor to Europe.

In addition to his job as a leatherworker, Paul worked tirelessly day and night, preaching, teaching, and writing letters to help the churches stay on track and be strong in the face of opposition. Hostility was vehement from both within and without. Within the church, false teachers fired their malignant darts in an attempt to pull the infant church away from the gospel message Paul had preached. From outside the church, social and political pressures and the pagan culture attempted to crush the new and struggling fellowships. Although the gospel message withstood this animosity, opposition finally caught up with Paul himself who used his right as a Roman citizen to have his case tried before Caesar.

In Rome, Paul stayed under house arrest for two years where he was able to continue a teaching and writing ministry. After this imprisonment he was probably released for a little while before being taken captive again and martyred during a heavy persecution launched against all Christians by the Roman emperor Nero. However, this persecution did not stop the spread of the gospel. Even when the persecution increased about twenty years later under the Roman emperor Domitian, who demanded that Christians call him lord (a title they reserved for Jesus alone), Rome could not stop the gospel. Willing to pay with their lives for the good news about Jesus Christ, Christians continued to preach about the grace of God and the presence of his kingdom.

The last book of the Bible speaks to the suffering that God's people often face. At a time when Christians served as prey for wild animals for the amusement of crowds of spectators throughout the Roman empire, the book of Revelation gave Christians a glimpse of what was to come. Suffering will not last forever! God will honor his promise and vindicate his people. He will create a new heaven and a new earth where all evil will be removed. Those who have received his Spirit and become a part of his people in this life will come to enjoy his full presence forever. The presence of God and the coming of his kingdom that is now experienced in part will then be experienced in full. Those who through faith in Jesus enjoy God's fellowship in this life will end up where humanity began, in the full presence of God where they will see him face to face. The story will end where it began—God and humans together in close fellowship.

* * * * *

Why tell this story? We tell this story because it is more than a story, even more than just a true story. It is THE story! It is a story that, better than any other story, makes sense of life. It gives coherence and structure to our understanding of the universe. It gives meaning to our experiences and direction to our decisions. It is a story that has the power to reestablish the true quality of the humanness of life. It is a story that refuses apathy! It

requests a hearing! It petitions to be internalized! It promises a life-changing encounter with God!

Our lives as human beings are made up of stories that have shaped, or are shaping, who we are. The story of the Bible has the power to make sense of all the other stories of your life. When it is internalized and it becomes your story, it gives meaning in the midst of meaninglessness and value in the midst of worthlessness. Your personal story will find grounding in creation, guidance in crises, re-formation in redemption, and direction in its destination. People become Christians when their own stories merge with, and are understood in the light of, God's story.

EPISODE 1   CREATION

ACT 1
THE STORY BEGINS
Genesis 1–2

Episodes 1–7
are written by
Terry G. Carter

My wife and I are big fans of HGTV. This compulsion no doubt arises from owning a house built in 1942, which is in constant need of maintenance or update. Shows like *Property Brothers* or *Kitchen Crashers* always intrigue us. The stars take a house or room that is in shambles, dream up a design, and then go for it. Normally this means gutting a room completely and creating something totally new. When the experts first look at the chaos of the chosen room and dream, we experience the beginning of the story, but the episode never ends there. Eventually (and in all cases at a ridiculously low cost in the real world) the envisioned room transforms into a beautiful space.

All beginnings imply a story that follows and an ultimate goal. God's story is a bit different from my illustration since he starts with nothing and brings about all things. However, God's action of creation is only the beginning of the redemption story that has an ultimate, glorious goal.

Genesis 1:1 states clearly: "In the beginning . . ." This statement starts God's story and looks forward to a final, completed end. As we begin in Genesis we must remember it is only the beginning and that God has a plan that will be played out through the rest of the Bible and is, in fact, still being played out. There is a past where God acted, a present where he acts, and a "not yet" time where God will act to consummate the story. Read the first chapters carefully as they will give clues to the coming episodes of God's wonderful story of redemption.

Step 1: Read the Story (Genesis 1–2)

Gen. 1:1–26
cf. *Telling God's Story,*
p. 27 (referred to here-
after as *TGS*)

Q   In what order did God create all things?

1. The heaven and the earth and then he said "let there be light and there was.

2. God created the sky

3. God created the land, the oceans and all the plants

4. God created the sun, moon, and the stars

5. God created the birds, fish, and other sea creatures

6. God created all the land animals and people

Q At the end of each day God declared the work to be good and at the end of sixth day he said it was very good. Why "very good" for humans?   Gen. 1:31

Humans were one of the pinicle things that God created and he knew that we would follow his word. We are an image of him

Q What did God do to make humans different from all other creatures?   Gen. 1:27–30; cf. *TGS*, pp. 24–25

1. Mankind serves as viceroy over creation

2. God made humans to be a family with him

3. human have a dignity and a unique relationship with God

Q Why did God create a woman?   Gen. 2:18–25; cf. *TGS*, p. 25

God created a woman to bond with a man to make families. Also she was meant to share the responsibilities of the man.

Gen. 1:28–30; 2:15–17;
cf. *TGS*, p. 26

Q   What tasks did God give to Adam and Eve?

E1
A1

God gave them the task of naming all of the things he had created.

Gen. 2:23–25;
cf. *TGS*, p. 25

Q   What does Genesis say about the closeness of the marriage relationship?

Marriage is a true bond of man and woman to form a society called a family.

Step 2: Find the Meaning of the Story

e.g., powerful;
cf. *TGS*, p. 23

Q   God is the main character of the Bible. Every part of the story tells us something about God. List all the characteristics of God you see in the creation story.

God exersiced himself as the Creator of all things. God also desplayed himself that he has the all power. What some believe took billions of years he created in 6 days.

Q   As you discovered in reading Genesis 1–2, God created all things in a sequence, or order. Although we may never know why God created in the order listed in Genesis 1, what do *you* think?

I think he created the things in the order that he did because it was right.

Q   In what ways do we use the word "day" in our conversations and how might our uses of "day" relate to the creation story?

I think there is a relationship between the days we use and the creation in that we get closer to him every day and create new ideas.

18

Q   Humans are the crown of God's creation! God created all people in his image. The phrase *image of God* implies that we are very different from all other creatures. What truths about humans are found in Genesis 1–2 that show our uniqueness?

e.g., commune with God; cf. *TGS*, pp. 25–26

> Genesis 1-2 shows man as having the power to think clearly and make descions. God gave a uniqueness in that we are made in the image of himself.

Step 3: Make the Story Your Own

Q   Should the truth revealed in the creation story make a practical difference in your everyday life? If so, how?

> Yes, I believe it does because it shows our true trust in god rather than the theories of scientists.

Q   Ecology, environmental concerns, and preservation are very important issues to some people. How does the creation story teach you to relate to the world of nature?

> It reminds us that God gave us the power to work with the world that he created and included would be maintaining it.

Q   Think about the people in your neighborhood or those you work with. As persons created in the image of God, how much do you respect and care for them as God's creation? Pick a person you don't always enjoy encountering and every time you see him this week say to yourself, "This person is made in God's image and has great value. God loves him and so will I."

> I think that we as man should have the respect of fellow man in that we are all created in the image of him and should embrace his love.

E1
A1

19

Q   Family is important to God. What can you do this week to strengthen, value, and encourage your family?

I can obey my parents and honor their commnads and I can fellowship with my brother to strengthen our bond.

Preparing for the Next Act

At the end of each day God declared the creation to be good. Everything was as it should be. Adam and Eve communed with God daily and performed the tasks given them. However, as creatures designed with freedom of will, humans could alter that situation. A tragic turn of events took place to destroy this garden utopia described in Genesis 1–2. Humans rebelled and therefore found themselves in need of redemption.

ACT 2
HUMANS REJECT GOD'S PLAN
Genesis 3

Some situations seem so perfect that it shocks us when they take a terrible turn. During the 1800s in America, various groups attempted to establish utopian communities. The leaders of these communities believed they understood the principles on which to form a perfect society. Strangely, groups like the Shakers and the Oneida communities each organized on obviously opposite ideals for perfection. Neither ever attained utopia. In both cases one could argue that the bad decisions and sinful nature of members and leaders caused the demise.

Genesis 1–2 records the creation of a perfect society by God. At the end of each day God declared it good, and after the creation of humans he declared it very good. Then bad decisions and rebellion by those created replaced the whole creation, including humans, under the influence of a horrible condition. It was a condition that humans could not remedy or solve. This condition is called *sin*. Read how Adam and Eve got themselves into such a deadly trap.

Step 1: Read the Story (Genesis 3)

Gen. 3:1–5;
cf. *TGS*, pp. 31–32

Q   What does Satan tell Eve to convince her to rebel against God?

1. Satan told eve that god had simply mispoken which was a lie.
2. Satan told Eve that God was selfish and wanted all the power to himself.
3. Satan mislead Eve into believing that nothing bad would happen from eating of the tree.

Q What exactly was the sin Adam and Eve committed?   Gen. 2:16-17

The actual sin that Adam and Eve committed was not trusting God and going back on their word with him.

Q List the consequences of sin for each of the players in the story.   cf. TGS, pp. 32-35

1. For both Adam and Eve
Guilt, Shame, Seperation from God, and Physical and Spiritual Death
2. For Satan
Crawl on the ground, and enevidebbly crushed in the End

3. For Eve
Pain in child birth, and Tension between marriage

4. For Adam
Cursed ground - creation no longer cooperates

Q How is God's mercy and grace evident in Genesis 3?

God extended his mercy and grace by giving humans a chance and crushing the devil in the End.

Q How did sin continue to grow according to Genesis 4–11?   cf. TGS, pp. 35-37

1. Gen. 4
Adam and Eves children Cain killed his brother Abel

2. Gen. 6-8
The Lord found the people of the earth corrupt and killed everyone but Noah.
3. Gen. 11
The people of Babel tryied to build a tower to the heavens so they could be as good as god.

E1
A2

Step 2: Find the Meaning of the Story

hint: see also James
1:14–15 and compare to
Gen. 3; cf. TGS, p. 32

Q   How does Satan tempt humans?

Satan tempts humans by using the doubt that is already estabished from the beginning.

cf. TGS, p. 34

Q   How did sin affect the relationship between God and humans?

God had made a covenant with the people and had trusted them and humans let him down. He was greatly saddened but through his grace he still love.

hint: Gen. 3:15;
cf. TGS, p. 33

Q   Clearly the events recorded in Genesis 3 indicate that humans are in trouble. How does the story hint that God will fix that problem?

In the story god gave Satan punishments and made a promise he will fall in the End.

Gen. 4–11; Rom. 3:23;
8:19–22

Q   How does sin affect the whole world?

Sin affects the whole world in that we are all decendents of Adam and born with sin that clouds the direct relationship we have with God.

Step 3: Make the Story Your Own

Q   How do your own selfish desires cause you to rebel against God?

I try to do it as little as possible, but sometimes my judgement is clouded by worldly pleasures.

Q   What evidence do you see every day that shows sin is still rampant in the world and people need redemption?

When you turn on the news and hear of all the people that have been murdered gives me evidence that sin is rampant in the world.

Q   Consider the people you know who are not believers. How
     does this story inform you on the way they see life and what
     they value?

They see their apathy towards god as nothing but it is
true sin and they have let satan take control and
they believe in the doubt that Eve did.

Preparing for the Next Act

Just when it looked as if all was lost, God stepped in with his sovereign
plan to solve the problem. Only God could remedy the sin issue by his
power, grace, and mercy. He chose to use one man to be the seed for a
future of salvation and hope. Out of this man's family comes the one to
bless all nations. God will call out and form a covenant with the man
named Abraham.

E1
A2

EPISODE 2   THE PLAN OF REDEMPTION

2

ACT 1
COVENANT AND PROMISE
Genesis 12–24

Often human beings—people like us—work themselves into a corner and are unable to extricate themselves. They need the help of someone else. One of my grandson's favorite books that we read to him often is titled *The Little Red Truck*. The truck is friendly and everyone likes him. He goes "beep" when he greets his friends. Then along comes an arrogant, pushy dump truck that gets himself stuck in the mud. The little red truck tries to help but he too gets stuck. Eventually it takes all the friends to get them out. They were helpless and needed one or many who were strong enough to solve the problem.

cf. *TGS*, p. 43 map "The Journey of Abraham"

Genesis 3 is the story of people getting deeply trapped in sin. Sin kills and separates. People were and are powerless to defeat it and its consequence, which is death. In the case of sin, not even other people can help. Only God can, and his salvation plan began with a man named Abraham. The rest of the story unfolds God's wonderful strategy that became for all humans the only hope.

Step 1: Read the Story (Genesis 12–24)

Gen. 12:1–4; cf. *TGS*, pp. 41–43

Q   God makes several promises to Abraham. List them.

1. Land

2. Great Name

3. Great Nation

24

4. Blessing

5. Protection

6. Blessing for all nations

Q   What positive traits do you find in the story of Abraham that indicate he was a good choice for the covenant?

Gen. 12; 13; 14; 18:16–23; 22; cf. TGS, pp. 44–45

Abraham amongst all of the people worshiping Sin, he was worshiping the one true god.

Q   What events in the story reveal that Abraham was a fallible human like all people?

Gen. 12:10–20; 16; 20; cf. TGS, pp. 45–46

In one story Abraham passed of his wife as his sister to save his own neck.

Q   What promise did God fulfill for Abraham that allowed the covenant to pass to the next generation?

Gen. 21; cf. TGS, p. 46

God had promised Abraham a great nation, and when he turned 100 Sarah had a baby boy named Isaac to carry on the blessing.

Q   What was Abraham's greatest act of obedience to God?

Gen. 22; cf. TGS, pp. 46–47

His greatest act of obedience was that when God told him to sacrifice his own son he would have done it.

Step 2: Find the Meaning of the Story

Q   What do we see in the covenant God made with Abraham that would indicate the redemption plan had commenced?

Gen. 12:1–4; cf. TGS, p. 42

All of the things that God had promised to Abraham came true if he followed his word.

Q   Does God fulfill all his promises to Abraham?

Think of the rest of the story

Yes God did fulfill all of his promises Abraham did not know when but he did.

E2
A1

25

e.g., Gen. 18; 22;
cf. *TGS*, pp. 46–47

Q   Even though Abraham made mistakes, God continually shows his mercy and faithfulness. What events in the story show God's mercy and faithfulness to Abraham?

E2
A1

Even with his lying to Sarah and having a child with Hagar, God still spoke to Abraham.

Q   What truth is God teaching us in the following stories:

Gen. 18:16–26

1. Sodom and Gomorrah

Wicked cities that God destroyed

Gen. 21:8–21

2. Hagar and Ishmael

Trust in God and he will keep his promises

Gen. 22:1–19

3. The sacrifice of Isaac

You must obey God even when it is hard and he will reward you.

Step 3: Make the Story Your Own

Q   What do you see in your own life that shows you have the kind of trust in God that Abraham exhibited? How can you increase that trust in God?

I see in my life that when I do what I know is right I feel like God rewards me for doing the right thing.

Q   What are you currently doing to make sure the covenant message of God is made known to all the nations of the world? To your own neighbors?

I am spreading the word to all my friends and attending bible studies to strengthen my faith and others.

Q   What promise(s) has God fulfilled in your life that prove he is trustworthy and constant?

I have faced many physical challenges in my life and God has always provided the tools to fight the challenges.

Preparing for the Next Act

God fulfilled his promises to Abraham. He showed him mercy, strength, and love. God gave Abraham a son named Isaac, allowing the covenant to pass to the next generation and providing the possibility of a great nation. The son will become the covenant bearer and through this family God will build a people, out of whom the covenant God will bless the entire world.

ACT 2
ISAAC, JACOB, AND JOSEPH
Genesis 24–50

On a shelf in my house sits a hundred-year-old clock passed down to me by my father. It had belonged to his father. Monetarily, the clock possesses no high value, but as a family heirloom it is important to me. It is part of the family history and story. I will pass it to my daughter and in turn I hope it becomes my grandson's property. Things like a hundred-year-old clock matter to people. Often valuable family businesses, talents, family history, and possessions pass from one generation to the other.

Abraham received the most special gift in the form of a redemptive covenant designed to touch the whole world. This gift passed from Abraham to Isaac, Jacob, and Joseph, until it was finally fulfilled in Jesus. Follow the covenant story as you continue the journey.

Step 1: Read the Story (Genesis 24–50)

Q Where did Abraham and Sarah find a wife for Isaac, and why there?

Gen. 24; cf. TGS, p. 49

> They found a wife for Isaac in her brother Laban lord and they did not want him with a Canaanite.

Q Rebekah received advance information about her pregnancy. What did God tell her, and what was unique about the birth?

Gen. 25:19–28; cf. TGS, p. 50

> God gave Rebekah a unique pregnancy in that she had twins. God promised however that one would always rule over the other.

Q How did Jacob, the younger son, end up with the blessing instead of Esau, the elder? What was the "blessing"?

Gen. 25:27–34; 27; cf. TGS, pp. 50–51; p. 50 sidebar "The Blessing or Birthright"

E2
A2

> Jacob persuaded Esau into the birthright and then also tricked Isaac into giving it to him. The blessing was always given to the first born.

27

Gen. 28:10–22; 29; 30:25–43; 32:24–32; 33; *cf. TGS, pp. 51–52*

Q Where did God renew the covenant with Jacob? What did God promise to Jacob? What did God do for Jacob to fulfill the promise?

E2
A2

God renewed the covenant with Jacob in the land of Laban. God promised Jacob many of the things that he had promised to Abraham. Jacob recieved many wives.

Gen. 37; *cf. TGS, pp. 54–56*

Q How did Joseph end up in Egypt? Why would his brothers treat him so badly?

Joesph was sold by his brothers into slavery. His brothers did not like him because he was not the first born but most loved.

Gen. 37; 39–41; *cf. TGS, pp. 54–56*

Q What bad things happened to Joseph that God eventually turned around for good?

Joesph was accused of attempted rape by the wife of pharoh and was thrown in jail. It was in jail that Joesph learned to read dreams.

Gen. 12:1–4; *cf. TGS, pp. 56–57*

Q How did Joseph's time in Egypt and Jacob's move to that country result in the fulfillment of God's promise to Abraham?

Because Jacob moved to Egypt they survived the famine and his sons created tribes that multituded the earth.

Step 2: Find the Meaning of the Story

Gen. 25:27–34; 27

Q Did Jacob and Rebekah do the right thing by deceiving Isaac concerning the blessing?

Some do believe and some do not because they did what God had promised but not through the actions of God.

Q What can we learn from a study of the character traits of Jacob, Esau, and Joseph—both good and bad?

1. Jacob

Good - respect and give compassion to Gods people and he will reward you.

Bad - One must have patience and not rush into things promised by the lord.

2. Esau

Good - not holding a grudge on his brother for all of those years (forgiving)

Bad - being folish for giving up his birth right for something as simple as soup.

3. Joseph

Good - never giving up in the faith of God even though going through hard times.

Bad - Joseph tricked his brothers into thinking it was for food but it was to meet him.

Q   How does God build a nation from Abraham's family?   Gen. 46–50; cf. TGS, pp. 56–57

Passing down the covenant through Abrahams children and grandchildren and they had great nations and repopulated the earth.

Step 3: Make the Story Your Own

Q   The story describes in some detail how much Jacob was willing to do to be reconciled to Esau. Why is forgiveness and acceptance so important to humans? With whom do you need to reconcile?

Forgiveness and acceptance is important to humans because we will always disagree, but we need to coexist. I try not to burn bridges but I have sinned and need to reconsile with God.

E2
A2

Q   The story is filled with indications that God works good out of bad for the people he loves. How has God turned bad things in your life into positive outcomes?

> In my past I have had bad things happen to me but god has given me experiences and the tools to go through life.

Q   What is the evidence in your life that you are committed to purity and faithfulness like Joseph was?

> There have been many bad influences throughout my life and I have chosen the path of God not sin.

Preparing for the Next Act

cf. *TGS*, p. 57 chart "Jacob's Sons and the 12 Tribes of Israel"

The family of Jacob landed in Egypt, which turned out to be both good and bad for them. During the centuries in Egypt, God built Jacob's family into a formidable nation of probably more than three million people. God continued to fulfill his covenant promises. He never forgot his people. The events moved the covenant story closer to its fulfillment. It is sometimes hard for us to see the big picture when looking at the details, but our sovereign God controls the story and moves it toward the goal: redemption.

EPISODE 3   THE FORMING OF A NATION: GOD'S PEOPLE AND THE LAW

ACT 1
MOSES AND THE DELIVERANCE
Exodus 1–15

When I was just a child, Marvel Comics launched characters like the Fantastic Four, and the Avengers, and Spider-Man. Later on, movies touted these characters as bigger-than-life heroes. The public loves a superhero. When people are in trouble, the superhero comes to the rescue.

In the biblical story there is really only one super character and that is God alone. When his people landed in troubled circumstances, God rescued them—either raising up a special leader or performing a miracle. Moses became the leader God used to lead his people out of slavery to a new life. The Hebrews found themselves in a desperate place and our covenant God never forgot his people.

Step 1: Read the Story (Exodus 1–15)

Q   How did the Hebrews end up as slaves in Egypt?   Exod. 1; cf. TGS, p. 61

The number of Hebrews grew and the pharoh feared that they would take over so he enslaved them.

Q   How does Moses become the man God uses to free his people?   Exod. 3–4; cf. TGS, pp. 64–65

Moses fled Egypt in fear of him getting caught for killing an egyptian. While in the desert God approached him as a buring bush.

Exod. 5:2; 7:14–11:10; cf. TGS, p. 67

Q   God used ten plagues to convince Pharaoh to let the Hebrews go. List the plagues. Why did God send plagues of this type on the Egyptians? (These same plagues later appear in the last book of the Bible—Revelation.)

E3
A1

1. Turing the Nile to blood

2. Frogs

3. Gnats

4. Flies

5. Killing of Livestock

6. Boils on Egyptians

7. Hailstorm

8. Locusts

9. Darkness over Egypt

10. Death of firstborn Sons

Exod. 12; cf. TGS, pp. 67–68, esp. sidebar "Passover Feast"

Q   What is Passover? What were the Hebrews told to do? How is it a celebration of salvation?

The passover was the final plague when God sent a death angel to kill the firstborn sons. The Hebrews were instructed to put lamb blood on their door frame. God used blood to save the Hebrews and he uses Jesus's blood to save us.

Q   After the Hebrews left, Pharaoh changed his mind and came   Exod. 14; cf. *TGS*, p. 69
after them. How did God save them yet again?

God parted the Red Sea for long enough for the Hebrews to cross and then crushed the Egyptain army.

Step 2: Find the Meaning of the Story

Q   God approached Moses because his people were in great need.   Exod. 3–4;
What reasons did God give to Moses for enlisting him? List the   cf. *TGS*, pp. 64–66
excuses Moses gives to God to avoid being sent.

God gave the task of saving the Hebrews and taking them back to Canaan to Moses. Moses gave many excuses including facing the pharoh and he did not have the time.

Q   The Egyptians worshiped almost everything from animals   cf. *TGS*, p. 67
to celestial bodies. Look at the list of plagues. What do you
think God is trying to say to both the Hebrews and Egyptians
through the plagues?

I believe that the plagues tell us that if you do not worship the one true God you will be tortured.

Q   The plagues only negatively affected which group? What truth   Exod. 7–11
does that convey to both Hebrews and Egyptians?

The plagues only affected the Egyptians. The truth that comes out of this is that the Hebrews were Gods people and the Egyptians did not believe

Q   What is a miracle? Many miracles are recorded in this story.   cf. *TGS*, p. 70
What elements make them miracles?

Miricles are truely magical acts of God. A miracle can only be explained as an act that can only be understood through God.

The top right has handwritten "E3 A2".

Q   What kinds of excuses do you give to use to avoid doing what you know you should?

The most common excuse that I have is that I am too busy and dont have time.

Q   How has God rescued you?

God has rescued me in many ways, but the most important to me is in my faith.

Q   We live in a world that serves many gods. What truths can you learn from the story of Moses as you try to proclaim the truth and live for God in this world?

I have great comfort in knowing the accounts of the story of moses could only happen through God.

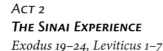

Preparing for the Next Act

The Hebrews were in Egypt for hundreds of years. In that time they lost their knowledge of and closeness to God. God was responsible for their growth. They were his people, but they really didn't know or understand that. They certainly didn't live like it. God used the wilderness and Sinai experience to teach them to be his people. Let's see how he accomplished that.

ACT 2

THE SINAI EXPERIENCE

Exodus 19–24, Leviticus 1–7

A new acquaintance recently shared with me that a mission trip had "rocked his world." He meant it was a highly significant event that changed his way of thinking and living. In other words, God really spoke to him in that event.

Mt. Sinai was that kind of event for the Hebrews, or at least it was intended to be. God brought the Hebrews to the mountain to show and teach them what being the people of God should look like. Unfortunately for the Hebrews, this event didn't impact them as it should have. That could not be due to unclear communication on God's part. He detailed

THE ROUTE OF THE EXODUS
EX 13:17–19:3;
NM 10:11–12:16; 33:1–36

Northern route
Central route
Alternate central route
Southern route
Alternate route from Jebel
Musa to Kadesh-barnea
● City
○ City (uncertain location)
▲ Mountain peak
▲ Possible locations for Mt. Sinai
Major roads

exactly what he expected of the Hebrews and how their corporate and individual lives should reflect their relationship with the God of the covenant. Let's see what God said to them at Sinai.

Step 1: Read the Story (Exodus 19–24)

Q   Name the ways God provided for and protected the Hebrews in the wilderness.

Exod. 15:22–27; 17
cf. *TGS*, pp. 73–75

God protected the Hebrews in many ways
including providing water, food when needed,
and success in battle.

Q   List the Ten Commandments as God gave them at Sinai.

1. Do not have other gods besides Me

2. Do not make an idol for yourself

3. Do not misuse the name of the Lord

4. Remember the Sabath day

5. Honor your father and your mother

6. Do not murder

7. Do not commit adultry

8. Do not steal

9. Do not give false testimony

10. Do not covet anything that belongs to Your neighbor.

Lev. 1–7   Q   What kind of sacrifices did God instruct the Hebrews to offer?

The burnt offering, the meal offering, the peace offering, the sin offering, and the trespass offering.

Q What was the role of the priests? What was the role of the High Priest, and who served in that position?   Exod. 28–30

The role of the priest was to give the sacrifices to God. The High Priest, Aaron, was the supreme religious leader of the Israelites.

Q Describe or draw the tabernacle. What was its purpose?   Exod. 26–27; 40:34–38; cf. *TGS*, pp. 80–81

The tabernacle was the tent of worship for the Israelites. It was surrounded by a court containing an altar for burnt offerings and a laver.

Q While Moses received the law on the mountain, what were the people doing at the base camp revealing they were a long way from being God's faithful people?   Exod. 32

The people pursuaded Aaron to build an altar of a cow for them to worship.

Step 2: Find the Meaning of the Story

Q God gives very specific instructions for collecting manna. What do you think God is trying to teach the people?   Exod. 16; cf. *TGS*, p. 73–75

Enjoy what you have and do not strive to have more than you need.

Q The Ten Commandments began with laws concerning a relationship with God. Why?   Exod. 20:1–17; cf. *TGS*, p. 77, esp. chart "Relationship with God"

A proper relationship with God sets the stage for all other relationships in life.

E3
A2

Lev. 1–7; Heb. 9:22;
Heb. 10:10

Q Why did God require blood sacrifices? What was God teaching and preparing the people for through these sacrifices?

The blood of all of these sacrifices is all teaching for the foreshadowing of the death of Jesus Christ.

Exod. 13:21–22;
40:34–48;
cf. *TGS*, pp. 80–81

Q By what means did God lead the people through the wilderness? Where did God dwell when they camped following the Sinai experience? Why is the presence of God such an important theological truth?

God lead the people on the path back toward the promised land of Canaan. God dwelt on the top of mount Sinai. When ever God is present he will take care of his people.

Gen. 12:1–4;
Exod. 20–24;
cf. *TGS*, pp. 78–79

Q Name three things that are different between the covenant that God gave to Abraham and the one he gave to Moses. Name one thing that is alike between the two covenants.

1. Different

Abrahamic: unilateral   Mosaic: bilateral

2. Different

Abrahamic–devine comitment   Mosaic–human obligation

3. Different

Abrahamic–restoration   Mosaic–judgement

4. Alike

Both meant to connect God with his people.

Step 3: Make the Story Your Own

Q How much time and attention each week do you spend on your relationship with God? What can you do this week to improve that focus?

I try to think of God in all that I do throughout the week. I could lessen the distraction of life and focus on him.

38

Q   The Ten Commandments provide timeless principles to guide our lives. Which of the commandments cause you the most trouble? What can you do this week to better live out those principles?

The main one that I have a problem with is coveting other peoples things. I should just rejoice in all that I have and not that what I don't.

Q   The presence of God marks the people of God. List the ways you have seen or experienced the presence of God this week.

This may sound silly but God has guided me through homework and the late nights to get the work done.

ABRAHAMIC COVENANT	MOSAIC COVENANT
one-sided, unilateral	two-sided, bilateral
"divine commitment" covenant	"human obligation" covenant
feature: God's promise	feature: man's obedience
result: restoration	result: judgment
NT term: grace	NT term: law

Preparing for the Next Act

After the journey to Sinai and the experience at the mountain, the Hebrews should have understood who God is and why they should follow and obey him. But humans are not always quick to learn. A bad decision at Kadesh Barnea led to a 38-year wandering and judgment. They continually struggled with submission to God's plan and to God as their master. The book of Numbers records that struggle.

E3
A2

ACT 3
THE WILDERNESS EXPERIENCE
Numbers 1–31

Some decisions in life plague us for years to come with regret and a desire for a do-over. As a teen I was a Boy Scout. I earned almost enough merit badges to reach the Eagle award. I served as Junior Assistant Scoutmaster, earned the God and Country Award, and was inducted into the Order of the Arrow. I scouted in a big way. Then I made a bad decision. I switched to an Explorer post thinking it meant more fun—at least that's what I thought. Our Explorer post did not emphasize advancement and I never earned another merit badge. I failed to reach Eagle Scout. I regret few things in my life, but that is one of them. It still haunts me.

At Kadesh Barnea the Hebrews made a bad choice not to trust God, and for the next 38 years, they surely regretted it. The book of Numbers continues the record of this arduous journey to the Promised Land.

Step 1: Read the Story (Numbers 1–31)

Num. 13–14;
cf. *TGS*, pp. 83–85

Q   What happened at Kadesh Barnea? What kind of land did the spies discover? Why was this event a turning point for the Hebrews, resulting in a 38-year wandering period? Who remained faithful and received exemption from the judgment?

At Kadesh Barnea, Moses sent spies into the Promised land to see how hard it was to conquer. 10 came back negative and 2 came back positive the People chose the negative and so they were banished except for Moses.

Num. 20; cf. *TGS*, p. 86

Q   What act resulted in Moses' being refused entry into the Promised Land after he had so faithfully led the rebellious people for so many years?

He was to make his staff make a rock produce water, but got so frustrated that he disobeyed God.

Num. 21:4–9;
cf. *TGS*, pp. 86–88

Q   The people rebelled repeatedly in the desert and God sent poisonous snakes to punish them. What was the solution to the snake problem?

The people were to obey god by when ever they got bit to look at the golden snake.

Q   In what way did God protect his people in the story of Balaam   Num. 22
and his donkey?

God prevented Balaam from cursing the people of Israel by sending an angel to stop his donkey.

Q   Numbers includes a census of the people before the journey   Num. 1; 26; cf. TGS, p. 88
in the wilderness and after. How many began and how many
ended? What is the difference between the two groups?

They started with 603,000 and ended with around 601,000 fighting men. The difference is that the new people trusted God.

Step 2: Find the Meaning of the Story

Q   How and what could the Hebrews learn through the repeated
judgments issued to them by God in the wilderness?

The hewbrews learned the hard way over and over again that you must trust God and believe in him.

Q   How is the Hebrews' behavior in the wilderness a picture of all
people to follow? In other words, how are they like most of us?

Like most of us today the Hebrews learned after the fact that they did the wrong thing.

Q   God offered a provision to take away the death caused by the   Num. 20; John 3:14; cf. TGS, p. 88
serpents. How is that a hint to the rest of the story?

God told the people that if they were bitten to look at the golden snake. This shows that even though they disobeyed him he still provides.

Q   Why would Moses be dealt such a harsh punishment for dis-   Num. 21; cf. TGS, p.86
obedience, even after having been so faithful?

Moses was dealt such a hard punishment because he was the leader of the Israelites.

E3
A3

Q Name several ways God's faithfulness to the covenant is evident in the wilderness travel? How is God's grace evident?

I think the biggest sign of grace was that god only banished the Israelites instead of killing them all.

Step 3: Make the Story Your Own

Q In your own life, how do you mimic the Hebrews' action and attitudes as they wandered through the wilderness?

I see this when I am really low because I tend to blame other things.

Q God's faithfulness and his care for you are evident every day of your life. List some examples.

I could not list all of the amazing things, but just a few would be getting to wake up, live a wonderful life, and praise him in the best way possible.

Q There are positive and negative characters in this part of the story. What truth can you learn from each of them to apply to your own life?

1. Caleb

Do not follow those that take the easy way

2. Joshua

The easy way is not always the best way

3. Aaron

Always trust in the lord and he will provide.

4. Moses

Even when others turn against God follow him.

5. Balaam

Know when you have met your match

6. Korah

Never oppose God or the leaders he has chosen.

Preparing for the Next Act

It's clear in the story that God is imminently more faithful and trust-worthy than the Hebrews. They constantly rebelled. They didn't deserve to enter the Promised Land. As promised by God, the generation that rebelled at Kadesh Barnea died in the wilderness. But God loved them still, and in fulfillment of his covenant led them to the land originally given to Abraham. The next generation enjoyed that blessing. Let's get them into Canaan—a land flowing with milk and honey.

E3
A3

EPISODE 4 THE PROMISED LAND AND SIN'S POWER

4

ACT 1
THE CONQUEST
Joshua 1–11

I enjoy seeing birthday celebrations that include a piñata. Usually it's full of candy, toys, and goodies that children love. However, the piñata does not yield its treasure without some exertion by the partygoers. They must whack at it until they bust it open. The prize hangs before them but requires action on their part.

God brought the Hebrews to the gate of the Promised Land for the second time (remember Kadesh Barnea). It lay before them, but God required some effort on their part: trust and fight. He ensured their victory when they trusted. In this process, God continued to teach them how to exercise faith and follow him as their one and only God. How well did they trust and obey?

Step 1: Read the Story (Joshua 1–11)

Deut. 34:1–4;
cf. *TGS*, p. 93

Q   Since God's punishment for Moses disallowed his entry into Canaan, what was he allowed to do?

He was allowed to choose his successor to lead his people into the promised land.

Josh. 1; cf. *TGS*, p. 93

Q   Who led the Hebrews into Canaan?

Joshua

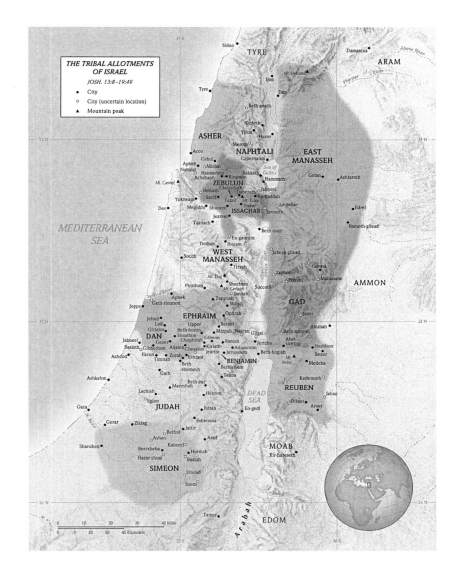

THE TRIBAL ALLOTMENTS
OF ISRAEL
JOSH. 13:8–19:49
• City
○ City (uncertain location)
▲ Mountain peak

Q   What miracle enabled the Hebrews to enter the Promised
    Land? To commemorate that feat, God instructed Joshua to do
    something as they crossed over the Jordan River into Canaan.
    What were the instructions?

Josh. 3–4;
cf. TGS, pp. 94–95

God parted the river of Jordan so the Israelite
could cross. They were to get 12 stones and
make a monument.

Q   How did God orchestrate the victory at Jericho?

Josh. 6;
cf. TGS, pp. 95–96

He instructed the people to walk around
the walls seven times on sevendays and then
sound and shout and the wall would fall.

E4
A1

Josh. 7;
cf. TGS, pp. 96–97

Q   The Hebrews lost the next battle at Ai. Who was to blame and what punishment did the sinner receive?

The Hebrews lost the battle because one man named Anchan took some gold.

Josh. 12–19;
cf. TGS, pp. 97–99

Q   How was the conquered land divided?

Some of the land had already been promised but the rest was divided between the 12 tribes.

Step 2: Find the Meaning of the Story

Josh. 4:4–7;
cf. TGS, pp. 94–95

Q   What purpose did the stone memorial serve? Why would that purpose be so important to the Hebrews after entering the Promised Land?

The memorial was to remind the people that God had done wonderful things for them. It would remind them to worship him and no others.

Josh. 6:22–27;
cf. Matt. 1:5;
cf. TGS, p. 95

Q   Rahab helps the Hebrews in the conquering of Jericho. What did God do for her to show her importance in the redemption story?

God let Rahab and her entire family survive and join the chosen people.

Josh. 7:16–26;
cf. TGS, p. 96–97

Q   Why would God punish all the Israelites with a defeat and all of Achan's family because of his personal sin?

The act of the one person meant that the whole group would be punished. The acts of one affected the whole group.

Q   Judging from the battles recorded in Joshua 1–11, whose power was responsible for the defeat of Canaan? Why was that so important for the Hebrews to understand?

Gods true power is the reason that the Hebrews won the day. The Hebrews could have never defeated Canaan by themselves without God.

46

Q   Why did God tell the Hebrews to kill all of the Canaanites—men, women, and children?

See Gen. 15:16;
cf. TGS, p. 100–2

God wanted to wipe the earth of nonbelievers and using the Hebrews to conquer the land.

CANAANITE FERTILITY WORSHIP

Fertility cults related to the changing of the seasons. Worshipers believed that the
sexual relationship of the gods caused good crops and therefore survival. Worship
participants sacrificed animals and sometimes even children. Their worship included
sexual immorality in order to please the gods. Jehovah, as the only true God, rejected
this sinful activity. The Hebrews were to avoid it and became God's instrument of
judgment on the Canaanites.

Step 3: Make the Story Your Own

Q   Why is it important for you to remember your own testimony
and the saving acts of God in your life? How are you passing
that story down to others?

Its fun to see how God works wonders in your life to prove that he provides for his people. It also satisfies the mind to hear of others to pass them down.

Q   What mistakes or bad decisions have you made that negatively
affected your family, friends, or church? How does the idea of
corporate responsibility relate to you?

I haven't done anything that has impacted my family but my brother lied one time and it reflected on the family.

E4
A1

> Q   The power of God served as the key element in the conquest. In what ways have you seen God's power in your own battles?

I have seen the power of God in my life through battles that I know I could not have won without his presence.

Preparing for the Next Act

God fulfilled his covenant promise. The Hebrews once again occupied Canaan. They were told to pass on the story of God's power and love to the generations to follow. They were also told to kill all the Canaanites as judgment for sin. How well did they accomplish these directions from God? The next part of the story makes the answer clear. We quickly see a turn for the worse in the story to come.

ACT 2
THE PERIOD OF THE JUDGES
Judges 1–16; Ruth

Between AD 500 and 1200, Europe experienced what has sometimes been called the Dark Ages. The term denotes a time of intellectual, cultural, and economic deterioration. It was not considered the best of times, although many believe some good things did happen during this period. For Israel, the Dark Age would clearly refer to the period when the judges ruled in Canaan. Shortly after the conquest, things began to fall apart. The command to pass from one generation to the next the story of God's covenant and the willingness to follow God alone grew less and less important to the people. The result was a repeating cycle of sin and rebellion. The story again takes a bad turn as it did in Genesis 3.

Step 1: Read the Story (Judges 1–16; Ruth)

Judg. 1

> Q   What did the Hebrews fail to do in the war that led to troubles from the Canaanites for years to come?

They failed to kill all of them and so there was always the presence of idols around the Hebrews.

Q   What was the cycle that the people of God repeatedly experi-
    enced as a result of their disobedience?

Judg. 2; cf. TGS, p. 106

The cycle that kept happening was that the
Hebrews sinned in some way and God sent
a judge to right it.

Q   Fill in the missing corresponding judge or foe found in the
    book of Judges.

Judg. 3–16;
cf. TGS, p. 108

JUDGE		FOE
Ehud	defeated	Eglon
Deborah and Barak	defeated	Canaanites
Gideon	defeated	Midianites and Amalekites
Samson	defeated	Philistines

Q   How did Deborah become the only woman judge? How was
    she helped by another woman in the event?

Judg. 4–5;
cf. TGS, pp. 107, 110

The male judges had flaws that made them
good candidates for judges in the story. The king
she was attempting to kill fled but was killed
by another woman.

Q   What made Gideon's victory so outstanding in military terms?
    Gideon had to be reassured for this battle. What did he ask
    God to do?

Judg. 6–7;
cf. TGS, pp. 110–11

God helped Gideon defeat a massive army
of 120,000 with only 300 men. He asked
God to lead the people rather than himself.

E4
A2

49

Judg. 13–16;
cf. *TGS*, pp. 111–12

Q What vow made Samson so strong, and how did he break every part of that vow?

Samson could not drink strong wine, Cut his hair, or touch anything unclean. He was takenover by flesh and did not protect the vow

Ruth; cf. Matt. 1:5;
cf. *TGS*, pp. 112–13

Q How is Ruth, a Moabite, incorporated into the Hebrews' story to become part of the lineage of Jesus?

It is from her and Boaz's lineage that King David and eventually Jesus comes from.

Step 2: Find the Meaning of the Story

cf. *TGS*, 106–7

Q Why did God allow the people to be oppressed by invaders over and over again?

The people of God turned away from him frequently and so he put them in check.

Q The judges were not always brave, moral followers of God. How would you characterize and describe the people God used to free the Hebrews from oppression? What lessons for the church do we find in these men?

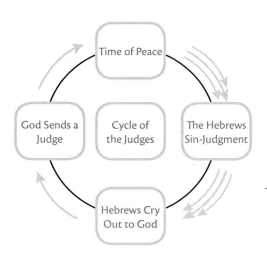

1. Gideon

Trust in God even when it seems that you are outmatched.

2. Jephthah

Trying your hardest and making Sacrifice to the lord pays off.

3. Samson

Even though we can get caught up in the world and with power, know that it can be lost very easily.

Q What does the period of the judges teach us about our covenant God and the way he deals with his people?

When Gods people are in need he sends extrodinary people to save them even when they dont deserve it.

Q During the time of the judges no one human ruler controlled the government. God served as the ruler. This is called a *theocracy*. Why did the Hebrews struggle with this?

Judg. 17:6; cf. TGS, p. 112

The Hebrew people struggled with sin because they had no central leader or direction so they sined.

Q Why is the story of Ruth so important to understanding the rest of the redemption story?

Ruth 4; cf. TGS, p. 113; see sidebar "Ancient Jewish Customs"

It is important to understand Ruth's story be cause her family will be made of King David and Jesus.

Step 3: Make the Story Your Own

Q In what ways do you see the cycle repeated during the time of the judges played out in your own life? What one spiritual principle can you see portrayed in this part of the story?

The cycle is seen in life because when we have bad times and ask him through prayer sometimes he sends ordinary people to make things right.

E4
A2

Q   The Hebrews were ruined by the idolatry that the Canaanites modeled for them. What kind of idolatry surrounds you daily that you must resist to remain faithful to God?

The most common type of idolatry is that God does not exist. I must remain strong and believe in him in the shadow of death.

Q   Ruth, Naomi, and Boaz exemplified some qualities that a Christian should possess. Identify these qualities. How are those evident in your life, and with which do you struggle to show?

Through all of these people I see a strong enflouence of others to enjoy and learn about God and I need to be better at speading his word.

Preparing for the Next Act

The people struggled under God's rule, committed idolatry, and participated in the immoral worship found in Canaanite fertility cults, which centered on the seasons of the year. Worshipers hoped to please Baal and thereby reap a good harvest. They believed that pleasing Baal would prompt good sexual relations between the god and his female counterpart, causing a fruitful crop yield. Worshipers committed immoral acts with temple prostitutes and priests as part of their ritual. When the Hebrews practiced these acts, they openly broke the covenant. In addition, they failed to pass down the truth of God to their children. Theocracy, the rule of God, didn't work out for them. As a result they eventually asked for another form of government. They sought to be like all the other nations. The nation changed drastically as they moved on from the period of the judges.

Episode 5   Israel Gets a King

5

Act 1
Samuel and Saul
1 Samuel 1–15

I know several people right now who are experiencing sad and tragic circumstances. These friends suffer not because of any decision or action they took. Life sometimes just proves to be hard. However, as believers, they know that eventually all bad things will end. They look to a better day when God will do away with their pain and suffering.

On the other hand, I know people who are suffering due to their own bad choices or sin. They brought the hardship on themselves. Yet sometimes, even for the guilty, God's grace intervenes to bring relief. They don't deserve that grace, but it comes anyway.

The period of the judges represents a dark time in Hebrew history filled with oppression and pain. That oppression grew out of the people's disobedience and sin. The Hebrews put themselves into the situation. God is just but also possesses covenant love and grace for his people; he revealed some clues to the merciful future in the story of Ruth. Then God raised up Samuel as the last judge before the Hebrews moved on to a new stage. Israel became a kingdom ruled by kings—some good and some bad. Eventually, God unfolds the promise of a messianic king, but the first king does not reflect messianic qualities.

Step 1: Read the Story (1 Samuel 1–15)

Q   What was unique to Samuel's birth and upbringing? How did it prepare him for his life's work?   1 Sam. 1–3; cf. TGS, p. 118

Samuel was born for the specific purpose of finding a king for Israel. He was trained as a Prophet, priest, and judge.

E5
A1

53

1 Sam. 2;
cf. *TGS*, pp. 117–18

Q   Why was Eli judged?

Eli was judged because his sons did wrong and turned away from God due to poor parenting from Eli.

1 Sam. 4–6;
cf. *TGS*, p. 119

Q   What happened to the ark of the covenant? Where was it, and what happened to those who possessed it?

During one of the battles with the Israelites the ark was taken to Palestine. God gave boils to the people that took it.

1 Sam. 8;
cf. *TGS*, pp. 119–21

Q   What reasons did the people give for wanting a king? What warnings did God tell Samuel to relay to the people?

The people wanted a king to get out from under theocracy but Samuel warned that eventually the people would not like a king.

1 Sam. 13–15;
cf. *TGS*, pp. 121–23

Q   Samuel selected Saul as the first king of Israel. Why did Samuel select him? Saul committed three sins and lost his kingdom. What were they?

Samuel selected Saul as king just cause he looked the part.

1. Usurped priestly role of sacrificing

2. Disregarding safety and well being of soldiers

3. Openly disobeyed God by refusing to kill the Amalekite king and keeping the spoils of war

Step 2: *Find the Meaning of the Story*

Q   Eli and Samuel served several roles. Eli served as priest and judge while Samuel served as priest, judge, and prophet. Describe the roles of a priest, judge, and prophet.

cf. TGS, p. 117

A priest is someone who conveys Gods message to the people. A judge is someone sent by God to Save the Israelits from sin. A prophet is a communicator between God and the people.

Q   Why would the people choose to have a king rather than continue under the theocracy (i.e., God's rule)?

1 Sam. 8;
cf. TGS, pp. 119–21

The people of Israel felt that God had not fulfilled their needs and they needed a king to move foreward.

Q   Why was Samuel so upset when Israel asked for a king? According to God, what did the request reveal about Israel?

1 Sam. 8:6–9

Samuel was upset because he believed that the people wanted to turn away from God. The request revealed that Israel had rejected God and no longer felt that he could rule them.

E5
A1

Q   Eli and Samuel raised rebellious children, which eventually cost them dearly. What spiritual truths can you learn from their stories? How important is a father's guidance?

The truths that come from that are that they were Godly men but were terrible parents. Children need a fathers guidance for direction.

Q   How do you reject God, preferring instead to be like others?

I try not to do this often but sometimes I do take the easier path instead of the one God has chosen for me.

Q   We learn from both good and bad characters in the biblical story. What can you learn from Eli, Samuel, or Saul?

I can learn from these men that it is very important to be a godly figure but also to raise children in his light.

Preparing for the Next Act

Saul proved a poor choice for king and struggled with Samuel's instructions constantly. In the end, God judged Saul's disobedience by withdrawing his Spirit from the king and taking away his kingdom. Samuel's task as an anointer of kings continued as he traveled to Jesse's home to find the successor to Saul. New criteria needed to be applied in the selection of the second king of Israel. This new king required a heart worthy of the title. Would Israel's next king fill the role more effectively? And how would God use this king to fulfill his covenant with his people?

Act 2

DAVID THE KING
1 Samuel 16–30; 2 Samuel 1–23

As I write this, the NFL draft looms only a few weeks away. Fans of struggling teams hope their teams draft that bigger-than-life, savior-of-the-program player. Many avid supporters of teams across the nation will gather in front of TVs or even make the trip to New York City just to observe the draft activities. In their minds, the team's whole future rests on the next pick. That player could make the difference between making the playoffs or not.

Because of Saul's inadequacies, the kingdom of Israel started slowly. A new king, a real difference-maker, was needed to fill the role. God's plan played out perfectly. The right pick waited in the fields of Jesse. God sent Samuel to select that king who would usher in a golden age for the Hebrews—one they refer to as the best of times. This king became the symbol of messianic hope. According to God, his dynasty would last forever.

Step 1: Read the Story (1 Samuel 16–30; 2 Samuel 1–23)

Q How was David selected and anointed as the new king by Samuel?

1 Sam. 16; cf. *TGS*, p. 125

David was chosen for other reasons rather than looks by God.

Q David rose to prominence with what event? What allowed David to be so bold and courageous?

1 Sam. 17; cf. *TGS*, p. 126

David was the only person that offered to take on Goliath and with Gods help he won.

Q How did Saul react to David's popularity? Conversely, how did David treat Saul?

1 Sam. 18–24

Saul felt very threatened by the uprising of David, but David knew he was to replace Saul.

Q God established a covenant with David. What did God promise him?

2 Sam. 7; cf. *TGS*, pp. 127–29

Even though David did not build to honor God God promised to give David honor.

E5
A2

57

2 Sam. 5–10

Q   Name three of David's notable accomplishments. Why would the people think he was a strong and faithful king?

E5
A2

1. David was successful in unifying Israel

2. He was successful in conquering Jerusalem

3. David brought the ark of the covenant into the capitol of Jerusalem.

2 Sam. 11–12;
cf. *TGS*, pp. 129–30

Q   Even though he was a good king, David stumbled due to his own sinfulness and humanity. What sins did he commit that caused God's prophet, Nathan, to judge him? What was the punishment?

David commited adultry with Bathseba and tried to cover it up by killing her husband. His punishment was that his son died just a few days after birth.

Step 2: Find the Meaning of the Story

1 Sam. 9; 16; cf. *TGS*,
p. 131 comparison chart
"David vs. Saul"

Q   What stands out as different between Samuel's selection of Saul and David? What does God want in a leader?

David was chosen by his heart rather than his looks. God wants good character in a leader

cf. *TGS*, pp. 127–29

Q   How does the story of Ruth relate to the covenant God established with David?

It is through David's line that God will redeem the sin of man.

1 Sam. 17; 24; 26;
2 Sam. 1; 6; 7:18–29; 22;
24:18–25

Q   What events in the story confirm that David desired to serve God?

David gave special care to the ark of the covenant in Jerusalem and admitted when he had done wrong and strived to fix it.

Q   The story refers to David as a "man after God's heart" and yet   2 Sam. 12:13–24;
    he commits some of the worst sins imaginable: adultery, deceit,   cf. *TGS*, pp. 130–31
    cover-up, and finally murder. How can he be called a "man
    after God's heart" with that record?

It may be hard to see a man after God's heart but David repents of his sins and tries to do everything he can to fix the problem.

Step 3: Make the Story Your Own

Q   When you consider your own heart, how worthy are you to
    be chosen by God for a special task? What needs to change in
    your life spiritually and morally?

I do not believe that any human being including myself are worthy of a special task but would love the oppertunity to serve the LORD in whatever way.

Q   The story of David teaches us about sin, repentance, and
    redemption. What sin in your life do you need to repent of, be
    forgiven by God, and cleansed by the Holy Spirit?

One sin that needs all of these things is in my times of weakness I do not come to him.

Q   How should you react to people who dislike you and seek to
    hurt you based on the life principles that David exhibited in
    his actions toward Saul?

You should treat these people with respect but know how to combat the threat the way God would want you too.

E5
A2

David served as the second king of the united kingdom of Israel. He made Jerusalem the capital, extended the kingdom to its largest size, and brought the ark of the covenant back to Israel. David received a messianic promise from God concerning his dynasty. Although good things happened during David's reign, the king also experienced the judgment of God because of his sin. He lost Bathsheba's first son. But God exercised mercy by allowing the second son of David and Bathsheba to reign. Everything appeared to be on a good track for Israel—and for a while it *was* good. But leaders sometimes fail to use all their faculties to serve the country well. God expected the kings of Israel to obey the covenant; he promised blessing for those who did and woe for those who didn't. The son of David took a detour into idolatry and set Israel's course in a new direction for the next several centuries.

EPISODE 6 REBELLION, JUDGMENT, AND FUTURE HOPE

6

ACT 1
SOLOMON AND THE DEMISE OF THE UNIFIED KINGDOM
1 Kings 3–12

I teach university students. Some of them struggle to grasp the material and pass the exams, while other students possess tremendous intellectual gifts, discipline, and an understanding of the concept of studying. I am never frustrated with either of these groups as long as they use their abilities to do their best. The students who frustrate me are those who have the gifts—sometimes remarkable gifts—and refuse to use them. They miss class, put in minimal effort, and end up with mediocre results. Blessed with great capacities, they squander their talents doing nothing, or even worse, doing the wrong things.

When young, inexperienced Solomon took the throne, God offered him a generous opportunity: "Ask what you will." Solomon asked for and received a great gift to help him better accomplish his new role as king. Yet in the end, he failed to use the gift and disaster ensued. It is a sad story of misplaced priorities and poor choices.

Step 1: Read the Story (1 Kings 3–12)

Q   What offer did God make to Solomon, and what did the young king choose?

1 Kings 3;
cf. TGS, pp. 135–37

The offer that God made to Solomon was the same as he gave david but Solomon chose to disoby god.

E6
A1

1 Kings 4–8; cf. *TGS*,
pp. 137–39; and p. 137
reconstruction of
Solomon's temple

Q What accomplishments are attributed to Solomon that demonstrate his great leadership as a king?

Instead of using force, Solomon relied heavily on relationships with other nations. Solomon also created a temple to hold the arc of the covenant.

1 Kings 11;
cf. *TGS*, pp. 139–40

Q What sins did Solomon commit, and what judgment did God inflict on him?

Solomon broke the first of the ten commandments when he chose the Gods of his many wives instead of the one true God. He was overthrown and dies shortly after.

1 Kings 11–12;
cf. *TGS*, pp. 140–42

Q Who rebelled against Solomon? What did God promise this rebel if he remained faithful to the covenant? What did this new leader do instead of following God?

Jeroboam rebeled against Solomon and overthrew him to take the promise of God. This new king did not however listen to the people of Israel which was against the covenant.

Step 2: Find the Meaning of the Story

1 Kings 3:16–28

Q What story does the Bible tell to demonstrate the gift Solomon received from God?

Solomon recieved the gift of wisdom because he was eager to follow in the ways of David.

Deut. 5: 8–10; 29:18;
1 Kings 11

Q The kings of Israel had one task—obey the Mosaic covenant. How did Solomon break it?

Solomon broke the Mosaic covenant by idolizing the gods of his wives instead of Yahweh

Q   What are the clues that Solomon's values were trending in the wrong direction during the building of the temple and his palace?   1 Kings 6:37–7:1; cf. TGS, p. 139

The temple and the palace turned out to be for worshiping other gods instead of God.

Q   What made Jeroboam rebel against Solomon? What act did Jeroboam commit to seal his rebellion against God and Israel?   1 Kings 11:26–40; cf. TGS, pp. 140–41

Jeroboam rebeled due to the high amount of taxes that Solomon had put on the people. While king he made the people work harder instead.

Q   What are the differences between Judah and Israel?   cf. TGS, p. 142

Judah had one dynasty under David while Israel had many. Judah had one Capitol to Israels three. Israel was always evil while Judah had good and evil.

JUDAH/SOUTHERN KINGDOM	ISRAEL/NORTHERN KINGDOM
One Dynasty—David	Nine Dynasties
One Capital—Jerusalem	Three Capitals— Shechem, Tirzah, Samaria
Good Kings / Evil Kings	All Evil Kings

Step 3: Make the Story Your Own

Q   What gifts do you possess that you have not used for God? How can you change that?

One gift that God gave me that I have not gotten to use much is helping others. I really need to get a job in my profession to do this.

E6
A1

Q   Solomon's values grew seriously out of whack. How about your values? Are the things of God more important to you than humanly prized things?

I think in my life the things of God are more important than human prized things at least I hope.

Q   Egypt negatively influenced Jeroboam to turn from God. How have the world and non-believers negatively affected you? Is it possible this influence exists and you are not even aware of it?

The world and non believers have tried their hardest to sway me and I try my hardest to fight it but there are some that you dont see.

Preparing for the Next Act

Solomon's sin earned God's judgment: division of the kingdom. Rehoboam, Solomon's son, took the throne of Judah and faced a rebellion led by Jeroboam, who ruled Israel. Soon after the division of the kingdom into Judah (southern kingdom) and Israel (northern kingdom) both slipped into rebellion. Israel slipped faster and more seriously due to its abundance of evil kings. Judah followed not far behind. Yet God never stopped loving his people in the north. He never quit pursuing them. God remains always faithful to his covenant even if people are miserable at keeping it.

God sent prophets who served as his spokesmen to bring the Hebrews back into covenant relationship. These men prophesied about the future (foretelling) but spent about 80% of their time preaching about current sin and rebellion (forthtelling, or preaching). Prophets called both Israel and Judah to return to their God. Their message sounded like a three-point sermon: 1. You have broken the covenant and need to repent. 2. If you refuse, God will judge you. 3. Even if God judges you, there is hope! They preached, performed miracles, used object lessons, and even tried poetry to get the message across. They highlighted the sins of idolatry, social injustice, and religious formalism. They reminded God's people of their covenant obligations. Sadly, in the northern kingdom of Israel, there is little evidence that any prophet succeeded. The slide toward judgment proved very quick indeed.

ACT 2
THE DEMISE OF THE NORTHERN KINGDOM
1 Kings 12 – 2 Kings 17; Amos; Hosea

I love golf. I was self-taught without any real understanding of the golf swing. As the game grew more important to me, I picked up classic golf swing books like Ben Hogan's *Five Lessons,* reading and marking the book repeatedly. It helped, but finally I felt the need to take lessons from a pro. The first lesson taught me the need to undo bad habits or swing practices. We all know the difficulty of ridding ourselves of a bad habit. Once a habit is formed, the wrong way begins to feel like the right way.

The northern kingdom of Israel started with the rebellion of Jeroboam. He refused to follow the covenant and receive God's blessing. Instead, he turned to idolatry and set the direction for all the northern kings to follow. One after the other walked in the ways of Jeroboam. The habit of sin and rebellion could not be broken and the descent to judgment was hastened. Israel only lasted only 200 years as a kingdom. God tried repeatedly to bring them back with powerful and colorful prophets, but their message landed on deaf ears. Disaster loomed.

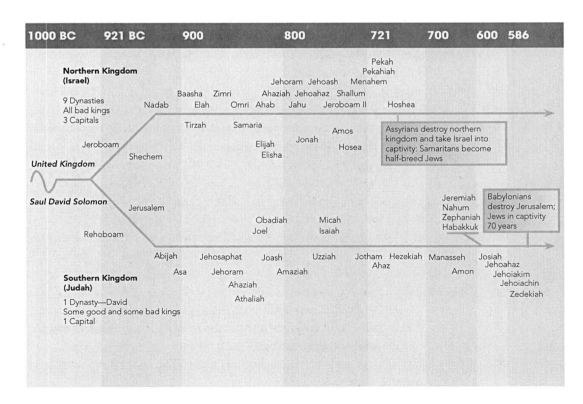

1 Kings 15:26, 34;
cf. 1 Kings 12:25–33;
cf. TGS, p. 151

Q   What sinful act did Jeroboam commit that set the pattern for all the leaders of Israel?

Jeroboam commited the sin of making idols of calves and other gods.

1 Kings 16:21–28;
cf. TGS, pp. 151–53

Q   Which king of Israel moved the capital to Samaria?

Omri

1 Kings 16:29–34;
cf. TGS, p. 153

Q   Which king of Israel accelerated the worship of Baal by marrying a foreign wife? What was her name, and what evil is she known for?

Ahab married Jezebel who worshiped Baal and brought her false god to Israel.

1 Kings 17–18;
cf. TGS, pp. 153–55

Q   What miracles did Elijah perform to show God's power to Ahab and the people of Israel? What happened at Mt. Carmel that proved God is the true God?

He challenged the worshipers of Baal and other gods to make a fire to burn up a offering.

1 Kings 19; cf. TGS, p. 156

Q   How did God minister to Elijah? What event taught Elijah that the one, sovereign God stood strong against the enemies of the prophet and controlled the future?

God ministered to Elijah not by great power in wind or earthquake but in a soft voice.

Q How does the story show the double portion of power Elisha possessed? What miracles did he perform?

2 Kings 2–6;
cf. TGS, pp. 156–58

Elisha had even more power than Elijah had. He helped make a miracle to cure a general of leprosy.

Q God sent two final prophets—Amos and Hosea—to call Israel back to the covenant. What was Amos' message to Israel? What judgment did the prophet reveal to the women? What hope did he offer to Israel?

Amos 3;
Amos 4;
Amos 5;
cf. TGS, pp. 158–59

Amos's message to Israel was that if they did not change their ways judgment would be on them. If the women did not help the children, widows, and old they would be hooked flesh

Q Hosea was the last prophet to Israel—a last chance from a merciful, covenant God. If Hosea's own life served as the model of his message to Israel, what did he teach? What was Hosea's one message to the northern kingdom?

Hos. 1–3;
Hos. 11;
cf. TGS, p. 159

Hosea's big message had to deal with adultry. His wife commited major adultry against him but he forgave her like God would do to israel.

Q The people never heeded the prophets' calls. Judgment came for breaking the covenant. How were they judged?

2 Kings 17:3–23;
cf. TGS, pp. 159–60

The people from the south invaded the north and destroyed Israel. The people were led away with hooks in their backs.

2 Kings 17:7–23

Q   Judgment came to Israel because of the people's sin. What were
     the sins of Israel?

Israel commited many sins including idolizing
false gods, not helping children and widows and
adultry.

Jer. 19:4–5;
cf. *TGS*, pp. 153–56

Q   Baal worship grew greatly in Israel from the beginning to the
     end. Who was Baal, and what was involved in the worship of
     Baal?

Baal was a false god that the nation
of Israel praised. They praised him by
worshiping idols looking like calves.

Q   God sent prophet after prophet to preach against sin and call
     Israel to repentance. What does that tell us about God? The
     people never responded to the prophets. What does that tell us
     about Israel?

The sending of many prophets shows how
much God loved Israel. The resentment
to the prophets tells us that Israel was weak minded.

2 Kings 17; cf. *TGS*, p. 160

Q   When judgment came to Israel, what happened to the ten
     tribes? What despised New Testament group grew up as a
     result of the exile and resettlement of Israel?

Judgement came and the ten tribes were broken
up later to form Samaritains and Gentiles.

Step 3: Make the Story Your Own

Q   What would a prophet of the Lord say to you concerning your
     relationship with God? Are any of the sins of Israel your sins?

A prophet from the Lord would tell me to
grow my faith to be stronger with him. I
would say not helping others as I should.

Q   It is clear that God continued to love Israel in spite of its sin. How do you see the love of God in your own life even when you sin and rebel?

Whenever I sin or rebel from the ways of God I am punished. The punishment is a sign of doing what is right not just continuing in sin.

Q   The prophets accused Israel of idolatry, social injustice, and religious formalism. How are those sins evident in the world today? What action can you take to reduce those practices in your own life and in the world in which you live?

The sins of Israel are very apparent today including idolizing other gods and social injustice among communities. One can reduce these things by trusting in the Lord and following only him.

Preparing for the Next Act

Every king in Israel was a bad king who did evil in the eyes of the Lord. The people followed their examples in spite of aggressive prophetic calls to righteousness. The end came in just two hundred years. God sent Assyria to brutally conquer Israel, and as Amos promised, the captives were led off by hooks attached to their flesh. The vicious Assyrians issued no mercy to captives. Israel received exactly what the prophets had promised for persisting in idolatry and social injustice. In 721 BC, that judgment came in full force. The ten tribes of the northern kingdom were pulled into captivity.

To the south, Judah struggled with the covenant demands as well. However, some good kings led Judah from time to time. The southern kingdom also responded to some prophetic calls to faithfulness. The road to final judgment moved more slowly in the south. However, the same sins plagued Judah and eventually the judgment rolled down. In the covenant, God promised blessing for faithfulness and woe for rebellion. Woe finally reached Judah.

ACT 3

THE SOUTHERN KINGDOM SLIDES

1 Kings 12 – 2 Kings 25

Christian history teaches us that religious fervor tends to rise and fall. A study of Christian awakenings through the centuries shows that spiritually, things get pretty bleak from time to time and then God raises up a person or persons to lead his people back in a revival movement. Occasionally the revival is dramatic and causes a major stir. Sometimes it is gradual and quieter. The same could be said of a spiritual decline.

Judah, the southern kingdom, experienced these spiritual ups and downs largely due to both good and bad leadership and the prophetic voices in its midst. The upright kings followed God's will and led the people to do likewise while other kings turned their backs on God and the covenant. Some of the prophetic messages landed on receptive hearts while at other times the soil was barren. As a result, religious decay slowed because of spurts of spiritual renewal. We observe this renewal with Hezekiah and Josiah. However, their faithfulness proved insufficient to stave off the coming judgment for the same sins Israel committed. Some of Judah's kings were every bit as bad as Jeroboam. The story of Manasseh alone shocks readers. Although traveling at a slower pace, God's judgment did eventually arrive in Judah.

Step 1: Read the Story (1 Kings 12 – 2 Kings 25)

1 Kings 12;
cf. TGS, pp. 140–42, 163

Q   Reheboam listened to bad advisors and the result was rebellion. What did Reheboam do to cause it?

He increased the taxes and hardship on the people.

Joel 1–2;
Joel 2:28–32;
cf. TGS, pp. 163–64

Q   Joel used what catastrophic natural disaster to convey the Lord's judgment for sin? What hope does Joel predict for the future?

Joel used locusts to convey the Lord's judgment for sin. Joel hoped that the Lord would pour his Spirit on the people.

Q   Isaiah made several messianic predictions. What are some of the most well-known and important of them?

Isa. 7; 9; 11; 53; cf. TGS, pp. 164–68

1. Birth of Jesus

2. Birth and Rule of Jesus

3. Future kingdom of Jesus

4. Sacrificial death of Jesus

Q   Isaiah prophesied under several kings. Some were receptive, while some were not. Name one king who refused to listen and one who heeded the prophet's advice.

Isa. 7; 36–40; 2 Kings 18–20

1. Rejected

Ahaz

2. Followed

Hezekiah

Q   Micah preached on the street to the common people. What was the theme of his prophecy?

Mic. 6:8; cf. TGS, p. 168

"He has told you men what is good and what the Lord requires of you: Only to act justly, love faithfulness, and walk with the Lord."

Q   Following Hezekiah, Judah fell quickly into idolatry and rebellion. Which king killed Isaiah? What other evil things did that king do?

2 Kings 21; cf. TGS, pp. 168–69

Manasseh killed Isaiah, established idolatry, and sacrificed his own children to pagan Gods.

Q   Josiah was a reforming king. What did Josiah do to try to bring Judah back to God?

2 Kings 22–23; cf. TGS, p. 169

Committed himself to God, destroyed Pagan temples, and found and reestablished the Covenant and law

E6
A3

2 Kings 23–24;
cf. *TGS*, pp. 169–70;
p. 170 chart "Judah's
Last Four Kings"

Q The last kings of Judah ignored God's covenant and led the people to destruction. Who were those kings, and who did God use to judge Judah?

E6
A3

Jehoabaz, Jehoiakim, Jehoiachin, and Zedekia. God used the prophets to judge Judah.

Step 2: Find the Meaning of the Story

2 Kings 18–19;
cf. *TGS*, p. 163

Q Why did the southern kingdom of Judah last longer than Israel to the north?

They had a mixture of good and evil kings instead of all evil.

Isa. 7; 9–11; Joel 2;
cf. *TGS*, pp. 164, 167

Q The main point of hope given by the prophets Joel and Isaiah focused on whom? Why can those who believe in God expect a bright eternal future?

The main hope was in Jesus and those who believe will dwell with him in the eternal kingdom.

cf. *TGS*, p. 169

Q What act of Josiah do you think stands out as most important for bringing the people back to God?

Finding the laws and reestablishing the covenant with God and people.

Acts 2; cf. *TGS*, p. 164

Q What New Testament event does Joel refer to in Joel 2:28–32?

Penecost

cf. *TGS*, p. 170

Q How could Judah have avoided invasion and destruction by Babylon? What were the prophets repeatedly trying to tell them?

Judah could have avoided invasion and destruction if they would have trusted in God as the prophets repeatedly told them.

Step 3: Make the Story Your Own

Q   How do Isaiah's prophecies concerning the Messiah affect
      your life personally? How does it bring you comfort, strength,
      and hope?

*It brings me great joy to know that
believing and trusting in God means that I
can dwell with him in heaven.*

Q   How earnestly do you listen to the preacher on Sunday and
      seek to incorporate biblical truth into your life?

*I try my very best to listen to what
the preacher says and implement it to my
life.*

Q   Joel prophesied about the coming of the Holy Spirit who
      would truly change people. How do you see the Holy Spirit at
      work in your life today?

*I see the Holy Spirit as the one that
is the voice in our heads telling us the
right thing to do in his eyes.*

Preparing for the Next Act

Judgment came, but God continued to speak to the people through the
prophets. Jeremiah spoke from Jerusalem to those facing the repeated invasions of the Babylonians. He even sent a letter to those taken away to
Babylon as captives. Nebuchadnezzar invaded Judah in 604 BC, taking
the finest young men like Daniel, Shadrach, Meshach, and Abednego off
to Babylon to serve him. Judah became a vassal state of Babylon. After
Judah rebelled against the Babylonians, Nebuchadnezzar returned again
in 597 BC, taking the king and Ezekiel, along with several other captives,
to live in Babylon. Finally, Nebuchadnezzar returned for the last time in
586 BC, totally destroying Jerusalem and transporting those not killed
into captivity. The misery persisted during the twenty years of invasions
and finally, all was lost. The story of these two decades makes up the next
act and tells us why they happened.

E6
A3

EPISODE 7   CAPTIVITY AND RETURN

7

ACT 1
THE JUDGMENT
Habakkuk, Jeremiah, Ezekiel

Life often seems unfair, especially if you judge it from a purely material-istic perspective. Sometimes very bad people become the wealthiest. The most unlikely character wins the big lottery, while others who feel more deserving don't. Conversely, very nice people find themselves without jobs and unable to cope. Why is this?

Habakkuk asked the same kind of question from a spiritual perspec-tive. Judah's sin reached the tipping point and judgment was imminent. God chose to use Babylon, an idolatrous, vicious people, to mete out that judgment. Habakkuk's mind just couldn't wrap around that idea. Why would an evil kingdom be punished by a seemingly more evil kingdom? He asked God and God's answer made sense. Babylon would get theirs, but first came Judah's turn. God is sovereign and Nebuchadnezzar became an unknowing instrument of judgment. The trauma began in 604 BC and ended in the total destruction of Jerusalem in 586. God is not mocked. He is just and he deals with sin. However, in the midst of it all, he continued to speak through his prophets of hope and a new covenant to come. Sin reaps death, but God never forgets his covenant people.

Step 1: Read the Story (Habakkuk, Jeremiah, Ezekiel)

Hab. 2;
cf. *TGS*, pp. 175–78

Q   What did God say to Habakkuk about the judgment of Judah?

That Babylon was going to destroy Judah, but Babylon would eventually get destroyed.

Jer. 36; cf. *TGS*, p. 178

Q   Jeremiah prophesied in Jerusalem during the reigns of the last four kings. He warned Jehoiakim of coming judgment

by delivering a scroll to him. What did the king do with the
scroll? How did Jeremiah respond?

*The king tore up and burned the
scroll. He dictated the scroll again and issued a statement.*

Q   Jeremiah also prophesied to the captives taken in 597 BC   Jer. 29;
through a letter found in Jeremiah 29: 1–14. According to the   cf. TGS, pp. 178–79
letter, how long could the captives expect to be in Babylon?
What does Jeremiah tell them to do while in captivity? Jeremiah ended with a message of hope. What is it?

*The people would be there a while
and to build families. There message
of hope was that the Promised land
would be returned.*

Q   Jeremiah and Ezekiel promised a new covenant for the future.   Jer. 31:32–33;
How is that covenant different from the Mosaic covenant?   Ezek. 36:26–28;
cf. TGS, pp. 179, 183

*This new covenant would be on the
hearts of the people rather than in stone.*

Q   Judah did not heed Jeremiah's message and destruction came.   Jer. 32; cf. TGS, p. 179
What did Nebuchadnezzar do in 586 BC? What unusual act
does Jeremiah perform to assure the people that there will be
a return?

*He leid siege to Jerusalem. Jeremiah bought
a piece of land in Judea as a sign of
return.*

Q   Ezekiel prophesied of the judgment while an exile with   Ezek. 4–5; cf. TGS, p. 181
the people. What strange things did he do to proclaim his
message?

*He cut off a third of his hair to those died by sword.
A third for the scattering of captivity. A third to those
who would die in famine and drought.*

cf. *TGS*, pp. 181–82

Q   Probably the most disturbing vision Ezekiel shared is found in Ezekiel 10. What was the vision, and what devastating truth did God teach the people through the vision?

Through this vision the people would look the presence of God.

cf. *TGS*, p. 182

Q   Ezekiel shared a message of hope through another vision in Ezekiel 37. What did it mean?

He promised that they would live and dwell in the Promised land again.

Step 2: *Find the Meaning of the Story*

Q   What does the whole story of the judgment of Judah say about God and his sovereignty?

He gives many chances, but is true to his Word on judgement. He still provides hope.

Jer. 29:10–14; Ezek. 37

Q   The very presence of the prophets Jeremiah and Ezekiel indicates that God is faithful to the covenant. What does each prophesy to assure the people that God does not forget his covenant even in the midst of sin and punishment?

They each prophesy that if the hold on and turn to him they can return someday.

John 3–4; Acts 2

Q   The new covenant prophesied in both Jeremiah and Ezekiel is fulfilled in what events in the New Testament?

In the new testament the people finally return to the promised land.

Amos 7–8

Q   Judah received judgment due to their actions and rebellious heart. What did they do to deserve it, and how did they treat God's prophets?

The people rejected the Gods prophets and did not worship the one true God.

Step 3: Make the Story Your Own

Q   God made promises to the Hebrews and kept them. What promises have you received from God, and why can you depend on God to keep them?

> I have recieved promesises from God that if I try my hadest he will find away. I will always deped on God for he is true.

Q   How does the new covenant promised by Jeremiah and Ezekiel relate to you? How do you experience it daily?

> The new covenant was placed on the hearts of the people and I feel that rather than commands set in stone.

Q   What have you done, said, or expressed by your attitude this week that reveals to others that God is sovereign and the future is in his hands?

> Many people are worried about their future life and money when God will provide to his people.

Preparing for the Next Act

Jeremiah promised seventy years in captivity. God always keeps his promises. Nebuchadnezzar, king of Babylon, conquered and transported Judah out of the Promised Land. During this time, Daniel and his companions served in the king's court. They remained faithful to God, and Daniel prophesied of the covenant love of God and messianic future awaiting his people. Eventually Persia conquered Babylon and set the stage for a return to the Promised Land. They returned in waves beginning in 536 BC. The question we now ask concerns the effect of the exile on the Hebrews. Did the people learn from their captivity? Did God and the covenant become more important to them?

Act 2
THE CAPTIVITY
Daniel 1–6; Jeremiah 29; Ezra 1

In *Gulliver's Travels,* Gulliver survives a shipwreck only to end up in a very strange land. Extremely small men tie him to the ground while he sleeps and he remains their captive for some time, even at one point being chained to a building. The new land proves strange in every possible way. As Gulliver continues to live with his captors, he learns about their culture, including an ongoing war. Although he doesn't want to get involved in the war, Gulliver offers his services to the emperor. *Gulliver's Travels* is a strange tale about a man held captive in an unknown land, trying to make the best of it.

cf. *TGS*, p. 186 sidebar "Jews"

Following the Babylonian victory, the Jews found themselves in a strange land among a different people. Promised it would last seventy years, they tried to make the best of a bad situation. Daniel and his companions served the king. Everyone coped while awaiting the return to their own land. The captivity demanded adaptation. The Jews struggled, yet amazing tales of faithfulness came out of that time. This narrative gives us courage, even today, when facing persecution and trial.

Step 1: Read the Story (Daniel 1–6; Jeremiah 29; Ezra 1)

Dan. 1; cf. *TGS*, p. 185

Q   When Nebuchadnezzar transported Daniel, Shadrach, Meshach, and Abednego to Babylon, what did he plan for them? How were they prepared for the task? What was Daniel's reaction and request?

Nebuchadnezzar planned for them to stay in the kings court. Daniel requested to only eat vegetables and thrived.

Dan. 3

Q   Shadrach, Meshach, and Abednego refused to bow to the statue set up for worship in Babylon. What was their punishment? How was God faithful?

The punishment was death by throwing them into the fiery furnace. God was faithful in keeping them alive in the furnace.

Q   Nebuchadnezzar dreamed of a statue made of several kinds of   Dan. 2; cf. TGS, p. 186
     metal.

     1. What is the statue?

     The statue was a man made of different metals.

     2. Daniel's interpretation?

     Daniel said that babylon was the feet and they would stand until crushed.

     3. Kingdoms to come?

     Babylon, Persia, Greece, and Rome

     4. Messianic prediction?

     Jesus would come twice to save those faithful to him.

Q   Which king rose to allow the Jews to return home? Who had   Ezra 1; Jer. 29; Ezek. 37;
     already predicted this return?   cf. TGS, pp. 187–88

     Cyrus the Great and Isaiah had already predicted
     the return.

Step 2: Find the Meaning of the Story

Q   What truth did Daniel reveal in Daniel 1 and 6 that would help
     future believers in times of difficulty and persecution?

     He revealed that those who remain faithful to
     God in times of difficulty would be cared for
     and recieve reward.

Q   What does Nebuchadnezzar's vision of the statue reveal about   Dan. 2
     God's sovereignty and his ultimate plan for humanity?

     The statue reveals to us that those who endangers
     and hold God's people captive will be judged
     and destroyed.

Q   God used two secular kings to accomplish his purposes: Ne-
     buchadnezzar and Cyrus. What does this teach us about God's
     ability to accomplish his purposes?

     This teaches us that God can use mighty and few
     people to make his point.

cf. *TGS*, p. 187

Q   How did the captivity help the Jews spiritually? How does it show that God can work good out of a bad situation?

Captivity helped the Jews because it made the turn to God instead of idols. This shows how when we are in dark time he cares for us.

Step 3: Make the Story Your Own

Q   How can you apply the experience and truths revealed in Daniel's experience in the lion's den? What about Shadrach, Meshach, and Abednego in the furnace?

It is easy to connect these experience into a lesson that can help us learn. When we are faced with persecution we must be faithful to him.

Q   Jesus clearly taught us that we do not know or control the future. How does the captivity story teach you to trust the future to God?

This captivity story lets you know that God has control of the future and if you trust in him he will do good for you.

Q   God cares for you every day in many ways. What are some ways that you know this is true?

He cares for me everyday by allowing me to live and be happy in life and provide protection against the devil.

Preparing for the Next Act

The covenant God loved his people, and just as he rescued them from Egypt, he rescued them from Babylon. Cyrus the Great conquered Babylon in 539 BC. An enlightened leader with different ideas on how to deal with captives, Cyrus allowed them to return to their homelands. Under his rule the Jews returned in waves to rebuild the temple, the city, and their lives as God's people. God used faithful leaders like Zerubbabel, Ezra, and Nehemiah to settle the Jews back into their homeland and call them to remember the covenant.

ACT 3
THE RETURN FROM EXILE AND THE REBUILDING OF THE TEMPLE
Ezra 1–5; Haggai; Zechariah

I have visited the ancient, ruined city of Pompeii several times. In AD 79, Vesuvius, the volcano that towered above the city, poured out ash and lava on this once-beautiful port, burying it and its inhabitants. An active, thriving community turned into a desolate wasteland in a matter of minutes. Of course, now Pompeii serves as a favorite tourist stop and is well worth the time. When walking the streets of the ruins, a traveler imagines what it must have been like in the days just prior to the volcanic eruption. Let's take that imagination in another direction. What would it have taken to restore the city to its former glory? It was never attempted. However, I'm sure survivors longed for Pompeii's old splendor.

Such a great task awaited the Jewish captives as they moved back to their beloved Jerusalem and the land promised to Abraham. At one time Jerusalem stood magnificently on the hill with its ornate temple and formidable walls. That picture became past tense for the Jews. Nebuchadnezzar had left no stone stacked on another. The desolation of 586 BC rendered the location barren with only memories of David and the stories of messianic glory. Beginning in 536 the Jews returned in waves. They found only the ruins of Jerusalem with little indication that it could be vital again. But God had a plan. He instructed Zerubbabel to rebuild the temple first. This took twenty years to complete, finally being rededicated in 516 BC. Rebuilding proved a hard task, with few available materials and other urgent needs occupying the minds of the returnees.

Step 1: Read the Story (Ezra 1–5, Haggai, Zechariah)

Ezra 1–3;
cf. *TGS*, pp. 191–92

Q   Who led the first returnees back to the spot where the ancient city of Jerusalem once stood? What priority task occupied the next several years?

Sheshbazzar led the first people back and the task was rebuilding the temple.

Ezra 4–5; Hag. 2;
cf. *TGS*, p. 193

Q   The rebuilding of the temple slowed for several reasons. What obstacles hindered the completion? What did the prophet Haggai say to get them working again?

Some of the people volunteered as workers to corrupt and some counceled against work. He told the people to work on the temple for God.

Zech. 9–10; 12–14;
cf. *TGS*, p. 193

Q   The building of the temple offered the opportunity for God's prophet Zechariah to look toward the future Messiah. Although not offering quite as many messianic predictions as Isaiah, a messianic theme nonetheless remains in Zechariah's message. What does Zechariah predict about Jerusalem and the future Messiah?

God was happy that the people finished the temple, but his presence must wait for the messiah.

Zech. 4

Q   For Zechariah, Zerubbabel occupies a special place in the story. What does the prophet say about Zerubbabel in the fourth chapter?

He was the prophet that brought the people out of exile and gowner of construction for the temple.

Step 2: Find the Meaning of the Story

Q   Why would God have the people returning from captivity build the temple first?

It was a sign of home and a dedication to put the works of God before thercoun.

Q   In both the tabernacle and Solomon's temple, the presence of the Lord resided in the Holy of Holies. At the rededication of the second temple in 516 BC, it was clear things were different. The presence of God would return, but when?

Zech. 9–10; cf. *TGS*, pp. 193–94

The presence of God in the second temple would have to wait for the Messiah.

Q   How would the preaching of Haggai be applicable to the church today since we are not building a temple?

Matt. 6:33–34

We must seek the kingdom of God and his richousness and he will provide for his people.

Step 3: Make the Story Your Own

Q   The Jews struggled with priorities. How do your priorities hinder you from following God's will?

I have a lot of work to do throughout the week and sometimes I put my freetime in place of Gods time.

Q   What did you learn about Jesus and the coming kingdom from Zechariah's prophecy?

I learned that God will make his presence known again and the people will follow him.

Q   In Solomon's temple, God dwelt in the Holy of Holies. Where does God dwell now on earth? Where is God's presence most powerfully exhibited?

John 14–16; 1 Cor. 6:19

God dwells with us in church, but his presence is most powefully exibited through prayer.

E7
A3

The Jews were now back in Jerusalem and worshiping again in the temple. It wasn't exactly Solomon's temple, but it served the purpose. Things began to look a little better, but the Jews were far from settled. Many who remained in Persia faced danger. A decree from the king condemned them to death, but the courage of Esther saved them. The Jews still lacked a few crucial pieces of the puzzle to really understand the concept of being God's people. The law still needed to be taught and adhered to if another judgment was to be avoided. Ezra returned to take care of that issue. Jerusalem stood exposed to enemies because the walls remained in shambles. Nehemiah led in this effort. Finally, one last prophet called the people of God to remember the covenant. The fulfillment of the promise of a Messiah—the solution to the sin problem—loomed in the near future. The story moved toward its climax.

ACT 4
REBUILDING JERUSALEM
Ezra 2–10; Esther; Nehemiah; Malachi

My wife and I are in the midst of remodeling a kitchen. The cabinets were installed this week, the floor lacks only the final coat of polyurethane, the windows stand ready for installation, and the crown molding waits to be mounted. We have reached the point of final touches. Actually much remains to be done, but compared to where we were in the beginning, we are definitely at the final touches phase.

The Jews returned under Zerubbabel and rebuilt the temple—a great start. But there were finishing touches to complete before the work ended. More people made their way out of captivity to the homeland. Reminders of covenant promises needed to be repeated and taught. The task remained unfinished until a wall stood against the enemies. God's promise was being fulfilled but there was still more of the story to unfold.

Step 1: Read the Story (Ezra 2–10; Esther; Nehemiah; Malachi)

Esther

> Q   What happened when King Xerxes replaced Queen Vashti? Who took her place, and why was that a providential blessing for the Jews?

Queen Vashti refused to go before the king so she was dethroned and replaced by King Artaxerxes who let the Jews return to Jerusalem.

Q Ezra returned with a large group in 457 BC. What constituted his main task?

Ezra's main task was to teach the people the Law of God.

Ezra 7; cf. *TGS*, p. 195

Q Nehemiah served in what position for King Artaxerxes? Why did Nehemiah return in 445 BC to Jerusalem? What was so amazing about his accomplishments?

Neh. 1–2; 4–6; cf. *TGS*, pp. 195–98

Nehemiah served as the cupbearer to the king. He returned to Jerusalem to help build a wall around the city. With help it was built in record time.

Q How did Nehemiah deal with opposition to the rebuilding of the wall?

Neh. 4; 6:1–14; cf. *TGS*, p. 198

While some workers worked on the wall, he stationed some with weapons to protect. His best help was the assurance he had in God.

Q Malachi is the last prophet of the Old Testament. What three sins does he focus on when preaching to the Jews?

cf. *TGS*, pp. 198–200

1. Mal. 1–2:10

Called out and warned disobedient priests

2. Mal. 2:13–17

Chastised Judah for material unfaithfulness

3. Mal. 3:6–18

Accused Judah of robbing from the tithe of God.

Q When Malachi referred to the Day of the Lord, was it a good thing or a bad thing?

Mal. 4

Malachi referred to the Day of the Lord as an awesome day.

E7
A4

cf. *TGS*, p. 195

Q   Why did Ezra focus so much on teaching and obeying the law? Why was that important for the Hebrews at this time in the story?

Ezra focused so much on the Law because that is what caused Judgment from God. It was important at this time because they had just returned and were weak.

Neh. 1: 4, 1:14; 2:11–20; 4:1–6, 4:13–14; 5: 1–13; 6: 9–14

Q   Nehemiah completed his task of rebuilding the wall in record time. How was this possible? What qualities did he possess to be so effective?

Nehemiah completed the task in record time due to the King and the assurance he had in God. God warned off the attackers and let the people work. His main qualities was his faithfulness to god and his leadership skills.

Q   The people still struggled with the covenant and its demands on their daily lives. What were the spiritual corrections that Malachi stressed to keep the Hebrews in line with God's will? How do preachers today preach like Malachi?

The main spiritual corrections that Malachi corrected was that of marrying foreign wives and making poor sacrifices. Preaches of today notice and know the greatest problems and try to correct us on those.

Step 3: Make the Story Your Own

Q   Is your attitude toward giving to God's causes what it should be, according to Malachi? Do you really trust God to bless you if you are faithful in giving?

I think that I could do better to give toward God's causes, but I try to do what I can. I whole heartedly trust that God will reward those that are faithful to him.

Q   What can you learn from Nehemiah that will help you in your
     walk as a believer? Where are you weak in your own character
     and efforts?

I can learn from Nehemiah that there
are going to be people who oppose God's way, but
he will protect you. I feel that I need to spend more time
with God weekly.

Q   Ezra 7:10 proclaims the motto of the leader's life. How seri-   cf. *TGS*, p. 200 chart
     ous are you at studying, obeying, and teaching God's truth?   "Political Power: Inter-
     What are you doing right now in your life that shows a   testamental Period"
     serious attitude?

I would say that I am upper tier on
the leadership of giving God's truth. I am
showing my seriousness in that I have spent
more time studying his word in the past year
than I have ever before.

THE STORY TO THIS POINT

Terry G. Carter

The whole story is God's story and he began it with the creation of all things—living and inanimate. Marked with the image of God and possessing a living soul, humans held the honored position of being the crown of that creation. They were created to fellowship with their creator, but instead they chose to disobey and make their own path. This decision resulted in separation from God and ultimately death. Humans found themselves in a predicament they could not remedy, but God had a gracious plan.

God formed a covenant with Abraham, promising a land, a great nation, and blessing for all nations of the world through the patriarch's family—a messianic promise. The Hebrews, tasked with blessing the world, proved to be an obstinate and rebellious group who ignored the covenant almost as often as they kept it. They experienced judgment, invasions, and finally captivity because of their sin. However, God never stopped loving them and always kept the covenant. He sent prophet after prophet to call them back and tell them of a wonderful future with the Messiah who would remedy the sin issue. Because they refused to follow, both kingdoms fell to invaders and captivity began.

God kept his promises, returning the Jews to Jerusalem and Palestine. They rebuilt the temple, refocused on the law, and raised the walls of the city again. The return set the stage for the fulfillment of the messianic appearance, which would come four hundred years after the last prophet Malachi reminded the people of covenant expectations. The next part of the story, found in the New Testament, offers the crescendo of the narrative with the birth, ministry, death, and resurrection of Jesus Christ, son of the living God.

During the four hundred years from Malachi to the birth of Christ, Palestine was ruled by three kingdoms. Following Persian rule, the Greeks, led by Alexander, conquered the world in the fourth century BC. In the first century BC a new power called Rome conquered Palestine. During this intertestamental time the Jews developed several cultural and religious characteristics that would figure heavily in the Gospel stories.

It was probably during the years of captivity, due to the absence of the temple and the need for a place to worship and teach God's word, that the synagogue was born. Key religious groups, centered on different goals and interests, developed during the period as well. The Sadducees grew in power to control the position of High Priest and rule the Sanhedrin, the council of seventy. The Pharisees took Ezra's focus on the law to heart and became the most committed devotees of it. Scribes transcribed and learned the law, earning the title of lawyer. Zealots emerged, desiring that all foreign oppression be forcibly removed, while on the opposite side of the political stage, publicans worked for the Romans collecting taxes and growing to be hated as traitors. Jesus was born into a legalistic, socially divided Jewish world.

POLITICAL POWER: INTERTESTAMENTAL PERIOD	
Persian Rule	539–323
Greek Rule	323–167
Jewish Independence	167–63
Roman Rule	63 through New Testament Period

E7
A4

8

EPISODE 8   UNTO US A CHILD IS BORN

ACT 1
GOD SENDS HIS PROMISED MESSIAH
Matthew 1–2; Luke 1–2

Episodes 8–14
are written by
Preben Vang

Have you ever longed for something with all your heart? Often excitement grows exponentially the closer the fulfillment of the goal seems. That's true whether it's a child who can't wait to see what a birthday or Christmas will bring or a student entering his or her senior year looking forward to the day of graduation. A couple in love counts the days until their wedding—and, they may count the days once again, when they are waiting to close on their first home. There are plenty of examples from daily life of the emotions that come with longing and true anticipation.

The people of Israel were in a similar emotional state as they awaited the arrival of Jesus. The prophetic promises given eight hundred years earlier by Isaiah, and those given by other prophets who prophesied about God's coming Messiah, still hung unfulfilled in the air. These prophesies were like stretched elastic bands ready to pull things back together. For four hundred years there had been no word from God to his people—four hundred long years between Malachi closing the book to the Old Testament and Matthew opening the story of the New Testament. The people were longing for the fulfillment of God's promise to send his Messiah.

The fulfillment begins in Matthew 1:1 with a reference to Abraham. What follows in the story of Jesus is the fulfillment of everything God has been revealing since establishing his covenant with Abraham in Genesis 12. The Gospel stories shout in harmony with the loudest voice possible: *Fulfillment!*

Step 1: Read the Story (Matt. 1–2; Luke 1–2)

Q   Which of the two Gospels tells us the story about Zechariah and John the Baptist?

Luke

Genesis 1–11 is about creation and fall (human rebellion).

Genesis 12 through Revelation is about God's
continuing work of redemption climaxing in Christ

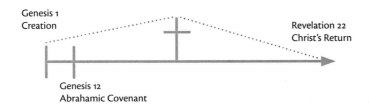

Genesis 1
Creation

Revelation 22
Christ's Return

Genesis 12
Abrahamic Covenant

Q   Which of the two Gospels records the song Mary sang when
visiting Elisabeth?

Luke

Q   Which of the two Gospels tells us about the magi?

Matthew

Q   How many magi does the Gospel say there were?

Maybe 3 no one noes.

Q   Which of the two Gospels tells us about the Roman emperor
Augustus?

Matthew

Q   In which Gospel are we told that Jesus' name shall be
Immanuel?

Matthew

Q   Which of the two Gospels tells us about Joseph's and Mary's
escape to Egypt?

Matthew

Q   Which of the two Gospels tells us the name of the angel
Gabriel?

Matthew

E8
A1

Q   Which of the two Gospels tells us about Jesus' circumcision in the Temple?

Luke

Q   Where do we hear about Jesus' visit to the temple as a 12-year-old?

Luke

Step 2: Find the Meaning of the Story

Q   Luke gives a clear historical marker by telling us that Jesus was born when Augustus was emperor in Rome. He ruled from 30 BC to AD 14. What other historical markers do we find in the two Gospel stories about Jesus' birth?

Destruction of the temple 70 AD

Herod the Great 37 BC to 4 BC

cf. *TGS*, pp. 214–18

Q   Galatians 4:4 and Ephesians 1:10 tell us that Jesus came in the "fullness of time." Other than this being the perfect time that God had decided to send his Son, what do you think this phrase could refer to? Anything happening in the world? Anything special related to the world situation and the Roman empire?

Jesus was sent when the people needed him the most. The expansion of roads made it easier to travel to other nations.

cf. *TGS*, p. 219

Q   We normally divide history into Before Christ (BC) and Anno Domini (AD). This division of the calendar was suggested by a monk named Dionysius in AD 525. From this, it should follow naturally that Jesus is born in the year zero. However, according to Matthew 2:1, Herod was ruling Judea when Jesus was born and we know from a number of other sources that Herod died in the year 4 BC. In light of Matthew 2:16, when do you think Jesus must have been born?

5 or 6 BC

Q   What does it tell you about the significance of Jesus when you notice who Matthew says he is the ultimate son of?

Matt. 1:1;
cf. *TGS*, pp. 220-1

> Matthew says that Jesus is the Son of Adam which tells us that he was sent for the people.

Q   How is your faith and understanding of Jesus affected since Luke's genealogy ends by calling Jesus the son of God?

Luke 3:38

> It just confirms the trinity of God the Father God the son, and God the Holy Ghost.

Q   What is the significance of Matthew calling Jesus Immanuel? What can you learn about this from reading Isaiah 7:14 and the surrounding verses?

Matt. 1:23

> The significance of Immanuel is that it means God with us. You can learn about how Jesus will save his people.

Q   What does it tell you about God's purposes that the angels announced Jesus' birth to poor shepherds on a field rather than influential leaders in Jerusalem?

> It shows that God is with the people not the rulers and how something amazing can come from nothing.

Q   Why do you think Matthew includes the story of the Gentile magi from the east?

> It shows that people came from very far to see the Messiah has been born.

Jesus' coming to earth as God's Son has so often been covered in pretty "Christmas wrapping" that it overshadows the true importance of the event. The situation for Joseph and Mary was extraordinarily difficult and is not well understood from the idyllic scenes often portrayed in various Christmas pageants. More importantly, the coming of Christ speaks to something very significant that we call *incarnation*. Without a sufficient understanding of the incarnation of Christ, we will miss the true importance of why God became human. In the next act, we will consider what it means that Jesus is the incarnation of God.

ACT 2
INCARNATION AND THE TWO NATURES OF JESUS
John 1:1–18; Galatians 4:4–5; Philippians 2:6–11

The word *incarnation* is not one most people use often in everyday speech. In fact, we use it so little that the word instead obtains prominence in non-Christian religions that affirm something called *reincarnation*. For example, Hinduism claims that souls are eternal and will be placed into new bodies when a person dies. After a person dies, he or she will come back (be re-incarnated) in another body either as another person, as some other creature, or as a spiritual being. How they come back depends on the moral quality of their previous life.

But, this notion is far from, and unrelated to, the meaning of incarnation in Christian teaching. *Carna* is a Latin word meaning flesh. When we say Christ is the incarnation of God, we simply affirm that he is God revealed in human form. Incarnation speaks to Jesus' human nature. He is not only 100% God, he is also 100% human just like you and me.

Incarnation is one of the most central doctrines of the Christian faith. It asserts that although Christ was with God from the beginning (equal with God), he took on human flesh and became like us. In this way God revealed himself to us on "our turf" so we can understand who he is and know what it means to be truly human in the way God intended it from the beginning.*

---

* For more on the extraordinary significance of this, see Preben Vang, "Incarnation," in *The Baker Illustrated Bible Dictionary*, ed. Tremper Longman III (Grand Rapids: Baker, 2013), 834–36.

Step 1: Read the Story (John 1:1–18; Galatians 4:4–5; Philippians 2:6–11)

Q   What does John 1:1 say about Jesus' nature as it relates to God the Father? Did God the Father exist before the Son?

In the beginning was the word and the word was God and they are three in one so they exist at the same time.

Q   What does John 1:3 say about Jesus' involvement in creation?

It says that all things were made by him and without him nothing would be made

Q   What does John 1:6–9 say about John the Baptist and how does it distinguish him from Jesus?

It says that John the Baptist is not the Light of the Lord but here to witness the Light.

Q   What does John 1:12 say about believers in Christ?

It says that the believers in christ recieve him and be called the Sons of God

Q   What does John 1:18 say about Jesus' relationship to the Father and the reason for his coming?

Jesus is the only man who has seen God and he was sent here to save his people from their sins.

Q   What does Philippians 2:6–7 say about Jesus' relationship to God?

Jesus is in the form of God but took upon the form of a servant like man.

Q   What does Philippians 2:8 say about Jesus' relationship to human beings?

He humbled himself to make himself a servant in the likeness of man

E8
A2

Q   According to Philippians 2:10–11, what opportunity does Jesus' dual nature (God and man) give human beings?

It says that all shall bow down to him and Confess their Sins to the Lord.

Q   How does Galatians 4:4–5 compare Jesus' situation to ours as human beings? What are the parallels?

God sent forth a son made of woman and of law to save the people made of Law.

Q   How does Galatians 4:4–5 explain the necessity of Jesus' incarnation?

It says that he was made by a woman but is sent to recieve sons.

Step 2: Find the Meaning of the Story

Q   How would you explain John 1:1–2 in light of Genesis 1:1–2?

It basicly explains that in the beggining he was the Word that was God.

Q   It's difficult for us as human beings to not think of a beginning for our existence (I did not exist 9+ months before I was born). How would you explain the relationship between the eternal Christ as described in John 1:1 and the historical Jesus as described in Luke 2:6–7 and 2:52?

The etranal christ is very God like while the historical Jesu is very much described as very humanlike.

Matt. 1:18–25;
Luke 1:26–38

Q   How does the story of the virgin birth of Christ connect to your answer above?

It shows that yes he was made inside a woman but was concieved by the Holy Spirit.

Q   How does Philippians 2:6–11 influence the way you think about Jesus as a human being?

It slow how truely incredible he is because he was a human being, but yet he was God and the people bowed down to him.

Q   Why do you think Paul highlighted that Jesus was born of a woman and born under the law?   Gal. 4:4

I think that he highlighted this fact because he wanted to demonstrate that Jesus had human form and the form of God.

Q   What are we losing as Christians when we don't highlight the incarnation?

When we lose the incarnation we lose that there was an actual human being that acted in the ways of God.

Step 3: Make the Story Your Own

Q   In light of the fact that God revealed himself through the incarnation of Christ, what does it mean for you to live an *incarnate* Christian life?

It means that you live a Christian life inspite of the sinful flesh.

Q   What needs to change in your life for this to become a reality?

For one to really live an incarnate Christian life one needs to only do what the Lord says and resist sin.

E8
A2

Q   Because Jesus is the Son of God, he can save you. What is the significance of Jesus' humanity for your daily life? What can you learn from the human Jesus?

Jesus' humanity is very important to me because through the study of his life one can learn how to live as a human.

Q   It is a temptation for believers to not consider the significance of Jesus' life and only focus on his death and resurrection. Jesus' life is reduced, then, to a matter of sinlessness (Jesus lived so that his sinless life could be used as a sacrifice to God for us). How would a greater emphasis on Jesus' life affect the way you understand the gospel message?

The gospel gives us a "good news" so then Jesus's life must means good news to people.

Q   The Gospels clearly spend most of their time talking about Jesus' life. How should this realization change the way you think about the gospel and the way you present the plan of salvation to others?

It is very important to know that God sent his only begotten Son to save his people from their sins.

Preparing for the Next Act

Reading a biography and studying someone's life can be an intriguing endeavor. Well-written biographies of highly known and influential people often become best sellers. Beyond what we may learn historically from reading about a well-known person's life, there's something about biographies that innately appeals to human interest. What was it that made these personalities stand out? What can we learn from looking at their lives? How can we find inspiration from their decisions and activities? Moreover, do their lives and their words have power to transform our lives if we listen carefully?

EPISODE 9　THE MINISTRY OF JESUS

ACT 1
JESUS BEGINS HIS MINISTRY
Matthew 3–4; Luke 3–5:11; John 1:19–51

Most biographies begin in a fashion similar to the description of Jesus in the so-called synoptic Gospels (Matthew, Mark, and Luke). After sufficient research, the author of a biography usually describes the family background, birthplace, and social setting of the person's life they describe. But that's where the comparison to the Synoptics ends. Unlike the three synoptic Gospels, a modern biography likely details a series of childhood events the author considers formative for the person's development and pertinent to the readers' understanding. In our modern era where psychological development, rather than family lineage, sets the stage for our understanding of personal development, upbringing demands a serious consideration.

The Gospels are biographies, but not in the modern sense of that term. We are told very little about Jesus' upbringing. We know he was the oldest son in a home where the father was a carpenter. This means that Jesus grew up in a middle-class home. A carpenter's job was to make and repair furniture as well as tools for farming and other occupations. At times, carpenters worked in stone and metal and could even fill the role of general contractor. As the oldest son, Jesus would have had a leading position in the family business. Luke 2:52 hints at Jesus' physical and intellectual development. A family visit to the temple in Jerusalem reveals that Jesus, at twelve years old, was extraordinarily gifted spiritually and intellectually (Luke 2:47).

The emphasis of all the Gospels is Jesus' public ministry, which began at his baptism.

E9
A1

Q   Which of the Gospels give us historical details about the Roman world that help us date when these events took place?

Matthew

Luke 3:1

Q   Who was the ruler of Galilee at that time?

Herod

Matt. 3:1–3; Luke 3:2–3

Q   What was the name of the person who was preaching in the desert of Judah before Jesus came on the scene?

John

Matt. 3:4; cf. *TGS*, p. 234

Q   His dress is likened to that of a prophet. How is it described?

John clothes were made of camels hair, and he had a leather belt around his waist.

Matt. 3:3; Luke 3:4; cf. *TGS*, p. 233

Q   Which Old Testament prophet had spoken about this person as a forerunner for Jesus?

Isaiah

Matt. 3:13; cf. Matt. 11:2–15; cf. *TGS*, p. 234

Q   Who baptized Jesus, and why is this significant?

John the Baptist Baptized Jesus and this is significant because it bridged old and new Covenant.

Q   Which of the Gospels tell us that Jesus was praying after he got baptized?

Mark

Matt. 3:17; Luke 3:22

Q   What did God say and do as Jesus was coming up from the water?

"He saw the heavens being torn open and the Spirit descending to him like a dove saying You are my beloved son; I take delight in you."

Matt. 4:1–2; Luke 4:1–2; cf. Mark 1:12–13; cf. *TGS*, p. 238

Q   After Jesus was baptized, he was tempted by the devil. How much time passed between Jesus' baptism and his temptations, and what did Jesus do during that time?

The devil tempted Jesus over 40 years and the Spirit led him to the wilderness.

Q How many temptations did Jesus encounter in the desert?

Three

Q Which of the Gospels tells us that Jesus went to the synagogue after his temptations?

Luke

Q Which Old Testament prophet did Jesus preach from at this worship service?

Luke 4:16–19

Isaiah

Q Which of the Gospels record Jesus telling the disciples they will become fishers of men?

Matthew

Q Which of the Gospels records the calling of Nathanael?

John 1

Step 2: Find the Meaning of the Story

Q Why do you think Jesus was baptized?

cf. TGS, pp. 234–38

I think that Jesus was baptized because it allowed him to connect to the sinfulness of man.

Q Sometimes a few words can function as a shorthand reference to something well known—"We the people" makes us think of the constitution; "Oh say can you see" makes us think of the national anthem. God similarly used well-known catch phrases as shorthand to say something important about Jesus.

1. Compare "this is my Son" to Psalm 2:7. Psalm 2 is a coronation hymn used when kings were installed. In light of this, what do you think this phrase means?

cf. TGS, p. 236

It is just saying that when the Holy Spirit sayed this it clarified that Jesus was king.

E9
A1

cf. TGS, p. 236

2. Compare "whom I love" to Genesis 22:2 and consider what God announced about Jesus in this statement.

This compares to Abraham when God asked him to sacrifice his son like God will.

cf. TGS, p. 236

3. Compare "with him I'm well pleased" to the servant hymn in Isaiah 42:1–9 and consider what you can learn about Jesus' ministry from this comparison.

It reminds us the suffering servant of God will reveal a new covenant.

Q   Jesus was tempted. What does it mean to be tempted?

Be in a situation that try to lure a person to do something sinful or wrong.

cf. TGS, p. 240–41

Q   What's the difference between a temptation and a test?

The diffence between temptation and test is that a test is generally refering to something good.

Q   If you were to explain what Jesus was going through in the wilderness, would you say Jesus was *tempted, tested,* or *tried*? Explain.

I think it was a test by God to make sure that Jesus could not sin.

Q   Jesus called twelve disciples. Why twelve? Why not seven, for example, which is also a common biblical number?

cf. *TGS*, p. 242 chart of the 12 disciples; and p. 243 on the significance of 12

12 is a reocurring number because it comes from the original 12 tribes.

Q   Can you think of any contrast of personalities among the disciples? Try to give at least one example.

Peter was impulsive Steadfast while the Other gospels were not.

Q   Why do you think Jesus called such a diverse group?

cf. *TGS*, p. 243–44

I think he did this so that his disciples could connect with people from all walks of life.

Step 3: *Make the Story Your Own*

Q   How can God's message at Jesus' baptism help you better understand not only what Jesus' ministry was all about, but also what it means to live the Christian life?

I think that the message at the baptism shows us that we all can be servants of God and are made for a purpose.

Q   Above you explained the difference in English between temptation, test, and trial. In Greek, the word *peirasmos* covers all three. Nothing in the text tells you how to translate it. In James 1:2, for example, it says, "consider it pure joy . . . when you face *peirasmos* of many kinds." How does this insight change the way you think about the difficult situations you meet? Are they temptations, tests, or trials? Think of a specific situation.

cf. *TGS*, p. 240–1

1.   In what way is it a temptation?

It is a temptation because it is the want to do sin that is not right.

E9
A1

103

2. In what way is it a test?

It would be a test because someone will always be watching to see what your response is.

3. In what way is it a trial?

It would be a trial because hopefully it would be a difficult choice in one mind.

cf. TGS, p. 243

Q Thinking about the reason for the *twelve* disciples, how does this help your understanding of what it means to be a disciple in relationship to the community we call the church?

To be a disciple to the church means that one should teach and learn the ways of the church to be a better servant of God.

cf. TGS, p. 243

Q Jesus called a rather motley crew of people to be his disciples. In what way does that inform your thinking about whom you should reach out to and help disciple?

It just shows that one should reach out to help all walks of life because every human battles with sin.

Preparing for the Next Act

Communication has become one of the most sought-after disciplines and skills in our modern day. Whether businesses are rethinking their public relations approach, politicians are planning their next campaign, universities are profiling their strengths, labels are starting a "re-branding" effort, churches are creating websites to attract visitors, or pastors are thinking about how best to present their message, great communication skills are central to capture the desired audiences and to ensure that the right message is heard.

Act 2
Jesus' Message and Methods
Mark 1–4; Matthew 5–7; Luke 10:25–11:54; 13–15; John 3–4

Jesus was a master communicator! His message was clear and precise. He used a variety of tools to communicate it to audiences of all sizes and backgrounds. The long-expected kingdom of God that prophets had announced would come at the end of time had now come near. God's presence would now again be visible among his people.

Preachers and Christians in general are rarely as clear as Jesus when they communicate the *main* message of the gospel. Often, if you ask people what they think Jesus' main message was, as they understand it from what they've heard in church or from friends, many will answer "love" or "grace." After all, Jesus told us to love one another—even our enemies (Matt 5:44). And, Jesus clearly taught that we are not saved by works but by grace (Matt 22:1–10; Luke 23:43). But, these are mere outflows of his *main* message. Jesus' main message is stated most succinctly in Mark 1:15: "Jesus came preaching the good news of God saying: 'The time is fulfilled, and the kingdom of God has come near; repent, and believe the good news.'"

Step 1: Read the Story (Matthew 5–7; Mark 1–4; Luke 10:25–11:54; 13–15; John 3–4)

Q   In Mark 1:15 there are two imperatives telling you what to do. What are they?

Repend and believe in the good news.

Q   Which of the Gospels records the Sermon on the Mount?

Matthew 5–7

Q   In Mark and Luke, Jesus uses the phrase "kingdom of God." What is the parallel phrase used by Matthew?

See, e.g., Matt. 3:2; 5:3, 10, 19; 13:10, 24, 31, 33

"kingdom of heaven"

E9
A2

Q   Which of the Gospels records the parable of the Good Samaritan?

Luke 10:25-37

Q   From the chapters you are reading for this section, which Gospel records the parable about the houses built on rock and on sand?

Matthew 7: 24-27

Matt. 6:22–24;
Mark 4:21–24;
Luke 8:16–18

Q   All three synoptic Gospels record the parable of the light under the bowl. How does the context where each Gospel author places the parable shed different light on its meaning?

The point in Matthew is to allow the goodness within you to produce good works to glorify God. And in Mark it means all things hidden and secret will be made known. Finally, Luke tells us what we allow to see affect the goodness within.

Q   Where do you find the Lord's Prayer in Matthew's Gospel?

Matthew 6:9-13

Q   Where do you find it in Luke's Gospel?

Luke 11

Q   How do the two differ?

Matthew was written on sermon on the Mount and thought inspiration while Luke was given to teach the disciples how to pray.

cf. TGS, p. 250

Q   Jesus' main message is that the kingdom of God has come near. What does the Lord's Prayer say about God's kingdom?

It says that thy kingdom come where all those that believe in him will live everlastly in his kingdom with him.

Q   How do the different petitions in the prayer speak to what
      Jesus means when he says "kingdom"?

*The kingdom parables are that of the prayer
Just to illustrate and describe what he meant
about the kingdom of God.*

Q   Which of the Gospels tells the story of Jesus' encounter with
      Nicodemus?

John 3:1-21

Q   Which of the Gospels tells the story of Jesus' meeting with the
      Samaritan woman at the well?

John 4

Q   What does this inclusion of the Samaritans say about the
      kingdom?

*It shows that all of God's people will
be able to live in the everlasting kingdom.*

Q   In Luke 14:1–14, Jesus was visited by a prominent Pharisee.
      What is Jesus teaching about the kingdom as they sat around
      the table?

*He teaches a very important lesson that
for all those who exalt themselves will be
humbled, and those who humble themselves
are exalted.*

Step 2: Find the Meaning of the Story

During the time of Jesus' ministry, the common Jewish belief was that
history is divided into two distinct periods. The present age is characterized by sin, sickness, and death—the absence of God's Spirit. The coming
age will begin when God fulfills his promise and comes back to restore
his kingdom on earth. This time will be characterized by righteousness,
wholeness, and everlasting life—the presence of God's Holy Spirit.

Jesus came to announce that the coming age has already begun, although it is not here in full. The present age still continues although the

cf. *TGS*, p. 245–48

E9
A2

kingdom is already revealed. The end of the present age and the fullness of the kingdom (coming age) will happen at Jesus' second coming. At that time "every knee shall bow" and "every tongue confess" (Phil. 2:10–11).

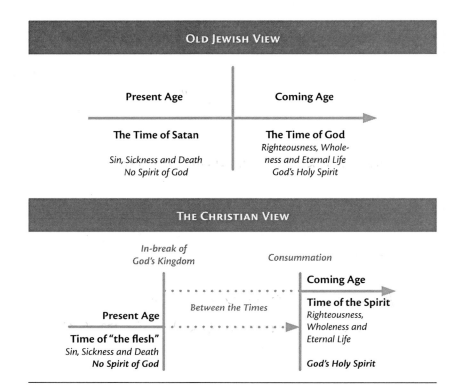

Q   What is the significance of Jesus' message that the kingdom has already come and is no longer just a future expectation?

The significance is that christains now know what to expect and that we know the kingdom is here.

cf. TGS, p. 248–50

Q   What do Luke 13:22–30 and 14:15–24 say about who will enter the kingdom of God?

Luke 13 suggests that you should take every measure you can to enter the kingdom. Luke 14 says those that rejected him opened the gate for others.

Q   Read Luke 18:9–14 and Matthew 18:1–5. What do these texts say about

     1. Repentance?

Those who humble themselves will get exalted and repentance

     2. Trust?

If you trust in the Lord then one can enter the kingdom.

Q   Jesus used parables to communicate the meaning of kingdom.   cf. Matt. 13:10–17
How would you explain what a parable is?

A story that is used to teach a lesson

Q   Every little element in a parable does not have meaning.   Luke 15:11–32;
There's generally one major point to a parable. Who's the   cf. TGS, p. 251–54
major character and what's the major point of the prodigal son
parable?

A man with two sons, one who gets inheritence and
speds it all foolishly and has to feed pigs and must
repent to recieve love from the father.

Q   What does this parable say about the kingdom of God?

God has opened the kingdom for all
to enjoy but we must return to him with humble hearts.

Q   What's the major point in the good Samaritan parable?   Luke 10:25–37

We should not only pray for our
enemies but also pray for them.

Q   What does this parable say about the kingdom of God?

The kingdom is going to be filled with
your friends and enemies and you should pray for them.

Q   What's the major point in the parable about the rich man and   Luke 16:19–31
Lazarus?

Those who are rich and love their money
neglect the law of justice, mercy, and faith.

E9
A2

cf. *TGS*, p. 255–56

Q   Jesus also used sermons to communicate his message. His longest sermon is found in Matthew 5–7. Jewish preachers spoke about keeping the law, but Jesus focused on internal attitudes that lead to actions. Give three examples from Matthew 5–7:

1. "Do not get angry"

2. "You shall not commit adultrey"

3. "Do not look at a woman with lust"

See, e.g., Matt. 16:13–16 and Mark 12:13–17; cf. *TGS*, pp. 256–57

Q   Jesus communicated through the use of questions. What is the strength of this approach to communication?

Using this method Jesus was able to let both his disciples and his opponents draw inescapeable conclusion about him.

Step 3: Make the Story Your Own

cf. Matt. 11:2–6; Luke 7:20–22

Q   Jesus said the kingdom has come near. "Near" can be both a temporal term (soon) and a spatial term (close/present). Many have read it in the temporal sense, but Jesus used it in the spatial sense. What practical difference does your understanding of "near" make in your daily application of Jesus' message?

Using in a temporal term is not good because soon is a relative term but Jesus meant that daily prayer will bring you closer.

Q   The kingdom petition in the Lord's Prayer is probably best understood as "may your kingdom be made visible among us." What does such a prayer mean when you pray it?

It means that when I pray I look forward to joining God in his kingdom soon.

Q Jesus' message is a call to his followers to become a part of God's kingdom. Obeying that call forces us to look away from our own preferences and focus on God's purposes for bringing his kingdom. How does that change your view of your daily tasks and your willingness to accept difficulties and suffering?

It changes my daily tasks in that instead of finding things that please me, I should be doing things that give glory to God.

Q Think of one or two confrontations you have had with people who you felt were attacking you. How would you have approached these situations differently if you had remembered Jesus' use of questions when people confronted him?

I would have approached these situations with less thoughts of revenge, but to help and pray for those people.

Preparing for the Next Act

It has become rather evident from the constant flow of stories in our national news media, which are presented as extraordinary events, that people's fascination with miracles is not diminishing. Uncommon and inexplicable events involving people who survive unusual circumstances, or the seemingly unending material for television series or movies relating to themes of the miraculous, or the huge sales of tabloids and other magazines that feature "unusual and abnormal happenings," highlight the continual interest in the extraordinary. In spite of our so-called scientific age, where we have an explanation for everything, people eagerly stand up to say, "I believe in miracles."

E9
A2

ACT 3
JESUS' MIRACLES AND MINISTRY
Matthew 8–9; Mark 5; John 2; 6; 9

The term "miracle," however, is very often ill defined. Sometimes it is used as a synonym for anything that is merely out of the ordinary. Sometimes it's a synonym for hope against all odds. At other times it is used to refer to something that disrupts the normal course of everything we know about the natural universe. Some speak of miracles in terms of a special timing (*amazingly, I received this news [or a check] just in time for me to avoid all these terrible things—it was a miracle*), a special experience (*this falling debris could have hit me and I would have been dead—it was a miracle*), or a special gratitude (*it's a miracle I wake up every morning and have strength to get out of bed*). Others reserve "miracle" for inexplicable happenings (*after we prayed for this person, the tumor was gone*).

cf. *TGS*, p. 260 (drawing)

When we talk about Jesus' miracles, we talk about miracles in the final sense listed above. A miracle related to Jesus, then, refers to the supernatural—that which goes beyond the mere natural and defies a natural or scientific explanation. It's an event that breaks the laws of nature as we know them and can only be explained as an intervention from God.

Step 1: Read the Story (Matthew 8–9; Mark 5; John 2; 6; 9)

Q   Which Gospel has the story about the faith of the Roman soldier?

Matthew 8:5-11

Matt. 8:5–13

Q   What was it that this centurion had understood about Jesus that Jesus did not find among the Israelites?

Jesus has the authority to do great things.

Q   Where do you find the story about Jesus changing water into wine?

John 2:1-11

Q   Where in the text readings listed above do you find Jesus cleansing the temple?

John 2: 13-22

Q   Which two Gospels tell the story of a girl being raised from the dead?

Mark and Matthew

Q   In both, that story is interrupted by another story sandwiched into the middle of it. What is that story about?

Matt. 9:18–26;
Mark 5:21–43

Jesus heals a sick woman

Q   John 9 is about the healing of what handicap?

Blindness

Q   What group of religious people was skeptical of Jesus' healing in that chapter?

The Pharisees

Q   Mark 5:1–20 tells the story of a demon exorcism. What happened to the demons?

The demons went out of the man and entered the pigs who ran in a lake to drown.

Q   Where in the text readings listed above does Jesus feed the 5,000?

John 6

Step 2: Find the Meaning of the Story

Q   Read Matthew 8:5–13, 23–27, Mark 5:1–18, and John 2:18. What common features do you see?

The most common feature that I see is that God through Jesus works miracles for his people.

Q   As mentioned above, two stories are sandwiched together in Matthew 9:18–26 and Mark 5:21–43. Stories are told a certain way for a reason. How do these two stories, when told in this way, shed light on each other and impact the meaning of each?

The big difference in the two is that the second time no one questioned the acts of Jesus and what he did.

E9
A3

Q   John often connects a concrete story to a teaching. How do you understand the connection between John 6:1–15 and 6:25–59?

The connection of Jesus feeding the 5,000 is that one should not work for food that spoils, but has eternal life.

Q   Consider the same for the connection between John 9:1–12 and 9:35–41.

Jesus says that the man was born blind so that God could do works on him. Jesus explained that those who were blind did not sin.

Q   How does the interjection of John 9:13–34 illustrate your conclusions above?

The Pharisees questioned Jesus healing and this points to not believing and seeing the Works of the Lord.

cf. *TGS*, p. 262–63 for a listing; 260–1 regarding the answer

Q   Jesus performed many miracles of different kinds. But what seems to be the focus and purpose of Jesus' miracles?

Just like Jesus parables he performs these miracles to teach a lesson.

Q   Just as Jesus' teaching was mostly related to certain social levels of society, so were his miracles.

1.   Which levels of society?

Most of Jesus miracles were related to the lower social class to the upper class.

2. Why do you think that is?

The lower society of people are the ones who trusted God, but the upper class are the ones who questioned his ways.

3. What does that say about the character of God's kingdom?

This shows that God's kingdom is open to all that are humble and have the ability to repent to him.

Q What do the miracles related directly to nature (like the stilling of the storm) show about Jesus?

Matt. 8:23–27;
Mark 4:35–41

The miracles of nature show us that not only does he have power over man, but he also has the power to control nature.

Q Jesus' miracles included quite a few demon exorcisms. What do they make evident in regard to God's kingdom?

Matt. 8:16–17; 8:28–34;
9:32–34; Mark 5:1–20

God's kingdom has no room for demons but does have room for the people haunted by them.

Q What do Jesus' healings convey about God's power?

Jesus's healings show that God has supreme power to do all things.

Step 3: Make the Story Your Own

Jesus' miracles were not stunts designed to get a following, to entertain people, or to make Jesus look like a powerful miracle worker. Rather they were teaching tools. Like Jesus' regular teaching, they were announcements about the coming of God's kingdom. They were evidence that what he said was true. God had come near. The effects of the fall—evil, sin, sickness, death—have lost their power. Where God's kingdom is evident,

cf. *TGS*, p. 259–61

E9
A3

people are set free, filled with joy, and given new life. Even nature itself will be released from its curse (cf. Rom. 8:20–22).

Q   How do you define miracle?

An extradirary work that could only be done by the Lord.

Q   How do Jesus' miracles strengthen your trust in God?

Jesus' miracles gives me strength to know that God will take care of his people.

Q   How do they help you see God's power and purpose in the world?

These miracles show power that man nor nature could do and signify that Gods purpose in the world.

Q   Are there any ways you can help people around you experience a miracle in their lives?

There are many things one could do to help those around like praying for them and helping wherever possible.

cf. TGS, p. 264–67

Q   Jesus seems to have had a special concern for the poor, the downtrodden, and the powerless. How does that impact your own life and ministry as a Christian?

That just shows that if Jesus had special concern for these people then I should as well in my Christian walk.

Q   Jesus cared extraordinarily for the sick, the ridiculed, and the
social outcasts. How does that relate to the way you spend
your time and effort? How can you better align what you teach
through your deeds with Jesus' deeds?

*This just shows that Jesus spent special
time with these people and that I should
probably do as well.*

Preparing for the Next Act

Sometimes events happen in such a way that everything gets lined up
(positively or negatively) for the perfect storm. Many people can attest
to that from personal experience. You may personally be able to as well.
Things and events that otherwise would have taken a long time to plan
and put in place can suddenly happen with rapid-fire speed. Doors open
and close in a way and with a speed that brings changes to your life so
quickly that it can seem as if you are becoming a mere spectator to your
destiny. In many ways this is the situation we find before the last week of
Jesus' life.

EPISODE 10 "A PROPHET MUST DIE IN JERUSALEM"

10

ACT 1
JESUS' ENTRY INTO JERUSALEM
Matthew 21; Mark 11; 14–15; Luke 19; John 12–13

Jesus' message about the arrival of the presence of God's kingdom among people was too great a challenge for the Jewish leadership to accept. The message of the nearness and nature of the kingdom proved to be an explicit indictment of almost everything that they claimed expressed godliness. The regular folks, in contrast, accepted Jesus' message and concluded that he may be the very Messiah promised by the prophets of old. Their longings and anticipations were finally finding fulfillment in Jesus. Jerusalem was abuzz! Something new and life-changing was about to happen.

cf. *TGS*, p. 272–73

Early in the week, most wanted to crown Jesus King of Israel; some, however, were already scheming to kill him.

Step 1: Read the Story (Matthew 21; Mark 11; 14–15; Luke 19; John 12–13)

Q   List the major events for each of the days we now call Holy Week.

Matt. 21:1–11;
Mark 11:1–11;
Luke 19:28–40;
John 12:12–19

1. Sunday:

Triumphal entry

Matt. 21:12–17;
Mark 11:15–18;
Luke 19:45–48;
John 2:12–24

2. Monday:

Cleansing of the temple

118

3. **Tuesday:**   Matt. 21:23–25:46;
                                                      Mark 11:27–13:37;
Teachings and parables   Luke 20:1–21:36

4. **Wednesday:**

No specific recordings

5. **Thursday:**   Matt. 26:17–30;
                                                      Mark 14:12–26;
- Passover   Luke 22:7–23;
- The Last Supper   John 13:1–30

6. **Friday:**   Matt. 27:1–66;
                                                      Mark 15:1–47;
Gethsemane   Luke 22:66–23:56;
arrest trial   John 18:28–19:37
Crusifixion, death
burial

7. **Saturday:**

Resurrection

8. **Sunday:**   Matt. 28:1–15;
                                                      Mark 16:1–20;
Further encounters   Luke 24:1–49;
                                                      John 20:1–31

E10
A1

Q How many of the Gospels describe Jesus' triumphal entry into Jerusalem?

four of them

Luke 19:1–8

Q Did Jesus encounter Zacchaeus before entering Jerusalem or in Jerusalem?

He encountered him before entering Jerusalem

Q What was Zacchaeus' job?

Chief tax collector in Jericho

Matt. 21:1–13;
Mark 11:1–3

Q On which mountain did the disciples get a donkey for Jesus to ride into Jerusalem?

The mount of olives

cf. *TGS*, p. 274

Q According to Matthew 21:11, how does the crowd identify Jesus?

They said that he was the phroplet of Nazereth of Galilee.

John 2:12–16;
Matt. 21:12–16;
Mark 11:15–18;
Luke 19:45–46

Q In terms of timing, how does John's explanation of the temple cleansing differ from the narrative in the other Gospels?

The difference is that John does not talk of Jesus healing people like the others.

Matt. 21:18–22;
Mark 11:12–14, 20–25;

Q Both Matthew and Mark intertwine a story about a fig tree that withers because Jesus curses it, with the story of Jesus' cleansing of the temple. How do they compare and differ?

They both say that Jesus saw no fruit so he cursed the tree, but Matthews story talks about the disciples choice of words.

Q Which of the Gospels tells the story of Jesus washing his disciples' feet?

John

Q Where does Jesus tell the parable of the two sons?

Matthew 21: 28-32

E10
A1

Step 2: Find the Meaning of the Story

Q   Consider the story of Zacchaeus and its placement in the Gospel story. What do you think is the significance of placing that story right before Jesus' entry into Jerusalem?

I think this story is a little bit of a foreshadowing of what Jesus is going to do in Jerusalem.

Q How does Zacchaeus' job and his response to Jesus play into the meaning of the bigger story told by the Gospel authors?

Being that Zacchaeus is a tax collector and Jesus speaks to him affirms that Jesus was going to save all people.

cf. TGS, p. 274

Q The triumphal entry is the fulfillment of Zechariah 9:9–10. What's the significance of Jesus riding on a donkey?

The entry on a donkey means that he was arriving with victory and peace.

cf. TGS, p. 273–74

Q Zechariah 14:1, 3–4 mentions the Mount of Olives in connection with end-time events. What significance does that have for our understanding of the story of Jesus' entry into Jerusalem?

It shows us that the Lords day is coming and that on that day he will stand on the mount of olives.

cf. TGS, p. 274

Q Read Leviticus 23:40 and Revelation 7:9. What do you learn about the meaning of palm branches in this context?

The cutting of the palm branches was a traditional Jewish way to celebrate God's rule and kingship.

John 2:12–16;
Matt. 21:12–26;
Mark 11:15–18;
Luke 19:45–46

Q How would you explain the difference between John's use of the temple cleansing event and the other Gospels' telling of this story? Does the use of this story in a different context change the meaning of the event for the readers?

John uses the cleansing of the temple like a parable to the disciples and I dont think it changes anything.

Q   From your notes above related to the fig tree and the temple   Matt. 21:18–22;
cleansing, explain how the "sandwiching" of these two sto-   Mark 11:12–14, 20–25
ries helps us better understand the meaning of the temple
cleansing event.

The sandwiching of these two stories
tells us that the cursed and money dwellers
will have no place in God's kingdom.

Q   How would you explain the prophetic indictment on external   cf. TGS, p. 276
religious formalism that is revealed in the fig tree incident?

I would say that if Jesus's word was
to curse you then there's a reason for so.

Step 3: Make the Story Your Own

The events of the days of Passion Week are important, not just for historical reasons, but for your own spiritual life. Answer the following questions
as you contemplate the meaning of the first few days.

Q   Palm Sunday is about celebration and crowning Jesus as King.
How does this influence the way you think about worship
gatherings and your participation in them?

I think this gives great hope for worship
gatherings and one should always participate.

Q   Practically, what do you think it means to call Jesus King?

To call Jesus king affirms that he will
be the ruler and guider of his people.

E10
A1

Q   Where do you need to strengthen your understanding and your Christian life to avoid hailing Jesus as King on Sunday only to risk crying, "Crucify him!" later in the week?

One needs to act the Godly way all week not just on Sunday.

Q   Monday is about cleaning the temple—making sure there's room for prayer and true devotion to God. What needs to be overturned or thrown out of your life to make room for that?

The main thing that needs to be thrown out of my life is ungodly sin.

Q   How will you go about making that happen?

I will make this happen by turning to God more than worldly pleasures.

Q   Tuesday is about being ready to give an answer when people ask you faith questions. How can you strengthen that ability in your own life?

I can strengthen that ability in my own life by reading the bible more.

Q   How does this relate to the amount of time you spend every week studying the Bible?

This matters alot in that reading the bible will help answer the questions.

Q   How does this relate to your involvement in evangelism (talking to non-believers about your faith) on a daily or weekly basis?

This means that evangelism should be happening more often throughout the week.

Q   Set an attainable six-month goal for the changes related to these questions that you want to see in your life. Then write it down here along with the process of how to get there.

To achieve these goals I plan to read and reach out to more people.

Preparing for the Next Act

Well-known and broadly celebrated events are usually filled with symbolic significance and a long history of memories. In America, this is true, for example, of Thanksgiving and the Fourth of July. Although many people celebrate these days without remembering the specific historical significance, they still often hold an important place in people's lives. As that holds true of national holidays, it proves even more true of religious holidays.

But when national or religious events are celebrated with full awareness of both their origin and their symbolic character, these events suddenly have an identity-shaping effect. Americans living overseas, for example, find a special bond—a sense of common identity—with other Americans celebrating the Fourth of July.

ACT 2
JESUS' LAST SUPPER AND CRUCIFIXION
Matthew 26–27; Luke 21–23; John 17–19; Romans 5

The Jewish Passover meal was especially designed to remind the people of their history and identity as a people (Exod. 12:2–3; Num. 9:2–3). In a very real sense, this was an identity-creating meal. As commanded in Deuteronomy 6:20–23 and Exodus 12:24–27, when the family is gathered around the table for the celebration of the Passover, a child will ask a question about why they are eating this special meal. The father will then tell the story of Exodus—*the* event that gives identity to the Jewish people. The coming generations will never need to question who they are or be in doubt about their identity.

Jesus took this meal and the elements used in it and re-interpreted everything in light of his own death on the cross (Luke 22:19; 1 Cor. 11:23–26).

E10
A2

The bread now refers to his body that was broken and the wine to his blood that was poured out. The celebration, then, of the Lord's Supper is an identity marker for Christians. It explains to us who we are as we understand our story in light of *his* story. The suffering, death, and resurrection of Christ is *the* event that gives meaning to everything else for a Christian. Christians do not need to struggle with identity crises. When people ask, "Who am I?" or "Who are you?" the answer comes back: "Let me tell you a story." It's the story that is rehearsed and retold every time Christians come together to celebrate the Lord's Supper.

Step 1: Read the Story (Matthew 26–27; Luke 21–23; John 17–19; Romans 5)

Q Where in the Gospels do we find a long prayer by Jesus that includes a prayer for those who have not yet heard the Good News?

Matthew

cf. TGS, p. 280

Q The similarities between the meaning of the Passover meal and the Lord's Supper are striking. The Passover reminds participants of the Abrahamic covenant. Which covenant does the Jesus speak about during the Lord's Supper?

He fulfills the Abrahamic covenant and tells of a new covenant in his blood

Matt. 26:31–34;
Luke 22:31–34

Q Jesus predicts that Peter will deny him before a certain time. When?

He predicts he will deny him three times.

John 2:19–21;
cf. Matt. 27:39

Q When Jesus said he would rebuild God's temple in three days, what was he talking about?

He was basically saying that he would reestablish God in the people in three days

Matt. 26:47–49;
Luke 22:47–48;
John 18:2–3

Q Which disciple betrayed Jesus?

Judas

John 18:10–11

Q Which of the disciples drew a sword to defend Jesus in the garden of Gethsemane?

Simon Peter

Q What was the name of the criminal the Jewish leadership asked Pilate to release instead of Jesus?

Luke 23:18–19; John 18:39–40

Barabbas

Q Jesus said to his mother, "Here's your son." Who took care of her after he died?

John 18:26–27

John

Q The Jewish leadership asked Pilate for permission to break the legs of the crucified, but they did not break Jesus' legs. Why not?

John 19:31–37

When the soldiers came to break his legs he was already dead.

Q What did the sign they hung on Jesus' cross say?

Matt. 27:37; Luke 23:18; John 19:19–22

Jesus of Nazareth the king of the Jews.

Q According to Romans 5:12–19, whom did Jesus die for?

He died to save the sins of all men

Q According to Romans 5:18–19, what is the result of Jesus' death?

That all men and sinners would become richoues.

Step 2: Find the Meaning of the Story

Q How would you explain Jesus' prayer and its placement in John 17? That is, how does its content influence how you understand chapters 18 and 19?

It is good placement so that those who have not heard the Good News will soon hear of it.

cf. *TGS*, pp. 279–83;
see chart on p. 280
"Parallels Between the
Passover and the Lord's
Supper"

Q Write down in your own words how Jesus reinterprets the
different elements of the Passover.

E10
A2

> Jesus fulfills covenant and makes a new
> One, Slavery is now in sin, Jesus will bring
> forgiveness, and the blood of Jesus passes our sin.

Matt. 26:6–13;
Luke 21:1–4

Q How do the narrations of the event in Simon the leper's house
and the story of the widow's mite inform the meaning of the
Passover story that follows?

> These stories further prove that the
> Passover and last supper have new
> meanings to the people.

John 18:12–24

Q John includes the story of violence on behalf of a disciple in
Gethsemane. How does Jesus' reaction to that help us better
understand the meaning of the cross?

> Jesus reaction is that of understanding
> that the event on the cross is important
> to the kingdom of God.

Q Explain the meaning of Paul's comparison of (or contrast between) Adam and Jesus in Romans 5:12–21.

> The main difference between Adam
> and Jesus is that Adam was good
> and turned evil when Jesus never sinned
> and was always good.

Step 3: Make the Story Your Own

Q   Jesus' prayer in John 17 includes you. Explain in what ways
      his prayer for you and for your testimony should impact your
      daily life as a Christian.

This prayer included us and that
is important because Jesus wanted
all of his people to be saved from
sin.

Q   The Old Testament salvation event is the Exodus. It is what the
      Jewish commemorate yearly as evidence that God remembers
      his covenant. It's their festival of redemption. Explain what you
      think "redemption" means.

Redemption to me means that the people
are going to be saved from sin.

Q   God chose to send his Son to die during the Passover celebra-
      tion, not on the great Day of Atonement (Yom Kippur). How
      does this timing impact your understanding of the cross and
      resurrection?

The timming tells me that the cross was
meant to save people and God for
the rest.

E10
A2

Q   How would its meaning have changed if Jesus had died on the Day of Atonement?

If Jesus had died on the Day of Atonement then there would be no hope left for Christians to follow.

Q   If you were to write a brief gospel tract, what you would write? Try to write one and share it with friends or a family members and ask them to respond.

If I was going to write a gospel tract, I would tell a story of how a man came to save all people.

Preparing for the Next Act

The mystery of death has always intrigued people. Why do we die? Is it possible to extend life and delay death? Is death the end of all things? If it is, does life itself make any sense? Why are we here if it all just stops and then . . . nothing? If it is not the end, what follows? Is what follows the same for everyone? Questions of all kinds relating to death and the afterlife have captivated human thinking since the earliest of times. Beyond that, there may be an even more perplexing question. Is there a chance that we will be raised from the dead and come back to experience a new kind of life with our loved ones and without the misery, pain, and difficulties we know from this life?

Answers to these questions have been manifold over the centuries. Some are the result of pure conjecture of personal wishes; some are the mere application of specific cultural experiences arising from various philosophical ideas; some are deeply rooted religious convictions; others again are simple empirical conclusions based on modern ideas about reality. Regardless of the continuing pressure from the latter of these, the constant flow of movies and TV shows broaching this subject reveals the depth of interest this topic continues to hold for most people. One current popular TV drama, *Resurrection*, imagines what would happen if people were raised back to life in our present reality.

Episode 11 The Grave Could Not Hold Him

11

MC

Act 1
Jesus' Burial and Resurrection
Matthew 28:1–15; Mark 16:1–8; Luke 24:1–12; John 20:1–9; 1 Corinthians 15

The Bible's message about Jesus rising from the dead on the third day has proven extraordinarily difficult to accept for many people. It is clearly a point of objection for modern (Western) people who are convinced that empirical evidence is the only worthy explanation of reality. Rather than being merely an objection in the modern period, however, the resurrection has caused great discussion throughout the centuries. Even Paul realized the need to address those who rejected the idea of resurrection from the dead. The Bible proclaims that death is the climactic result of sin and rebellion against God (Gen. 3). To enable a restoration between God and humans, God sent his Son, who reversed this curse not only by dying on our behalf, but by rising from the dead and thereby breaking death's power. Because death's power has now been broken, all who are in Christ will be raised to spend eternity with him. According to Paul, the resurrection is so central to Christian doctrine that the Christian faith stands or falls with the truth of it (1 Cor. 15:14–22).

Step 1: Read the Story (Matthew 28:1–15; Mark 16:1–8; Luke 24:1–12; John 20:1–9; 1 Cor. 15)

Q   How does Matthew explain that the stone was removed from the entrance to Jesus' tomb?

Matt. 28:2

He explains that the stone looked like it had been moved from the inside.

Mark 16:2–5; Luke 24:2; John 20:1

Q   What do the other three Gospels say about the way the stone is rolled away?

They said that it was incredible that the stone had been moved.

Q   According to each Gospel writer, who were the first to come to the tomb to witness the resurrection?

1.   Matthew 28:1

Two women

2.   Mark 16:1–3

Peter

3.   Luke 24:1, 10

Two women

4.   John 20:1

Peter

Matt. 28:5–7; Mark 16:5–7; Luke 24:4–7

Q   What does the angel announcing the resurrection say about Jesus?

She says that Jesus has risen to save everyone from their sins.

Q   Which Gospel highlights that the risen Jesus meets the women before he meets the disciples?

Matthew

cf. TGS, p. 306

Q   In 1 Corinthians 15:5–9, how many post-resurrection appearances does Paul list?

There are 3 mentioned

Q   Paul gives the shortest of summaries of the gospel message in 1 Corinthians 15:3–4—something he passed on as of *first* importance. List the elements that accordingly must be included in a gospel presentation:

Life, the death, the resurrection, and experiences.

Q   According to 1 Corinthians 15:35–54, what will happen to the natural body at resurrection?

It will stay on earth while the spiritual goes to heaven.

Q   Shall flesh and blood inherit the kingdom of God?   1 Cor. 15:50

No

Step 2: Find the Meaning of the Story

Q   Given that the testimony of women was not admissible as evidence at that time, how would you explain that the Gospels place women as the first witnesses to the resurrection?

Gospel puts women there to show a change in trust among people.

Q   In light of Matthew's story about the soldiers being paid off to say Jesus' body was stolen, how would you explain Luke's and John's emphasis on Peter finding the empty linen cloth?   Matt. 28:11–15; Luke 24:12; John 20:3–8

While the others thought someone had stole the body, he knew it was God.

Q   How would you argue today that it is highly unlikely that Jesus' body was stolen from the tomb?   cf. *TGS*, pp. 299–302

There is no concrete evidence that it was stolen.

Q Do you think the Gospels' emphasis that even those whose testimony was considered unusable could become primary witnesses for Christ has any significance for today? Explain.

Yes, it shows that even those who were not trusted, will be with God.

Q How does that impact the way you listen to testimonies from other people?

It makes me take them with a grain of salt knowing the truth.

cf. *TGS*, pp. 298–302; esp. p. 299 sidebar "Six Objections to Jesus' Resurrection"

Q What are some of the objections you have heard, or may have yourself, against Jesus' resurrection being a real historical event? How would you answer them if the people you talk to don't believe the Bible?

These accusations have no grounds while the bible has grounds of truth.

Q In 1 Corinthians 15, Paul says that all believers shall be raised. Using his imagery, how would you, in your own words, explain the connection between death and resurrection?

Death is the natural body and resurrection is the spiritual.

Q   When do you think the resurrection of believers will oc-   1 Cor. 15:20–23
     cur—at the death of the individual, or at the time of Christ's
     return? Explain.

At the time of Jesus return because that
is what is told.

Preparing for the Next Act

In most people's minds there's likely a distinction between the words "commission" and "command." The latter refers to a clear statement that must be obeyed. A parent says to a child, "Eat your vegetables." A ranking officer tells a soldier, "Go do this." A teacher tells a student, "Study more, if you want better grades." We may even use the phrase "She commands a lot of respect," meaning her presence has authority that compels others to follow her lead.

Commission, however, is usually taken as a broader charge to accomplish certain things according to a particular purpose. It's an authorization of sorts to make something happen. The notion of command is implied, but in a broader or softer way. A foundation can commission a work of art for a building. A city council can commission the development of a certain urban project. Used as a noun, a commission can simply be a committee with authority in a specific direction. But regardless of which term is used, neither "command" nor "commission" means "suggestion."

ACT 2
JESUS' POST-RESURRECTION APPEARANCES AND ASCENSION
Matthew 28:16–20; Luke 24:13–53; John 20:10–21; Acts 1:1–11

In English, we often refer to Matthew 28:19–20 as the Great Commission. In other languages, however, this text is called the Great Mission Commandment. In the Greek text, Jesus uses one imperative to charge (and/or command) his followers to continue his ministry after his ascension. To accomplish this, he promises to send his Spirit to enable and empower believers for the task. To grasp the full meaning of Matthew 28:19–20, it proves helpful to keep both terms discussed above in mind. Jesus commissions his followers—gives them a task to accomplish—by giving them a specific command to obey. This command is followed by a promise that when they obey this command, his presence will empower them to accomplish what he as their Lord has commissioned to be their purpose as his followers.

E11
A2

135

↓ Going

MAKE DISCIPLES of all nations

↑ ↑
| |
| Baptizing—in the name of the Father and the Son and the Holy Spirit
|
└── Teaching—all that I have commanded you

There is only **one** command—MAKE DISCIPLES;
going, baptizing, and teaching are modifiers that explain **how**!

Step 1: Read the Story (*Matthew 28:16–20; Luke 24:13–53; John 20:10–21; Acts 1:1–11*)

Q   Which Gospel tells the story about the walk to Emmaus?

Mark

Luke 24:28–31

Q   How (or at what point) did the disciples recognize Jesus in Emmaus?

They recognized him in the book of Luke.

John 20:10–18

Q   In John, which Mary is the first to see the resurrected Jesus?

Mary of Joseph

Q   Which Gospel tells the story of doubting Thomas?

John

Matt. 28:10, 16–18

Q   In Matthew, how many times does Jesus appear to his disciples before he gives the Great Commission?

two

cf. *TGS*, pp. 307–8

Q   In Matthew 28:19–20, how many imperatives (commands) do you see in your English translation? List the words in the imperative.

3 the blood, the body, the spirit

Luke 1:1

Q   To whom is Luke writing Acts?

The church

136

Q   What was the purpose of Jesus' post-resurrection appearances?   Acts 1:3

To validate that he is the Son of God

Q   Where were the disciples supposed to wait for the outpouring   Acts 1:4
     of the Spirit?

Jerusalem

Q   If Acts 1:8 is a short geographical summary of Matthew
     28:19–20, where does Jesus send his disciples first?

Jerusalem

Q   Explain in your own words how Jesus ascended.   Acts 1:9–11

He died and then in the night God came and rose him.

Q   What did the angels say about the way Jesus will come back?   Acts 1:10–11

They said he will come back with triumphal entry.

Step 2: Find the Meaning of the Story

Q   Explain in your own words the significance of Jesus' many   cf. TGS, p. 306 for a list-
     post-resurrection appearances and the variety of the settings   ing of Jesus' appearings
     in which they occurred.

The appearances were all for a reason and they all happened like they were miracles.

Q   Translating a text smoothly from one language to another can   cf. TGS, pp. 307–8
     be difficult. In the Greek text, how many imperatives (com-
     mands) are found in the Great Commission?

There are two

Q   Explain how this discovery changes your thinking about the charge Jesus gave his followers.

It just affirms that we should all speak and know the truest original text.

Matt. 28:20;
cf. *TGS*, p. 308

Q   What is the promise Jesus gives in the Great Commission?

He promises to save his people from their sins.

cf. *TGS*, pp. 308–9

Q   Explain how you understand the connection between Matthew 28:19–20, John 20:21–23, and Acts 1:8.

They are all related because they all are apperences that happend for a reason.

Acts 1:9–11;
cf. *TGS*, pp. 308–9

Q   Explain the meaning of Jesus' ascension. What was the purpose, and why was it necessary?

It was necessary to show the people that God was in control.

cf. *TGS*, pp. 309–10

Q   In the words of C. S. Lewis, Jesus is either a liar, lunatic, or Lord. Explain his argument.

Each of these points is a view of what some think of Jesus' teachings.

Step 3: Make the Story Your Own

Q   Christians often say that history is important, but in reality many tend not to care about historical issues of faith. How would you say the Gospels' emphasis on the post-resurrection appearances (Jesus did not just rise in the heart of the believers, but in actual bodily form) should impact your personal approach to Bible study?

This is a very important moment in time and should not be taken badly but a sign of hope.

Q   From another angle, how should this impact your pursuit of holiness—your desire to "see" the risen Lord?   e.g., Acts 7:55–56

It makes the story a little less believable to one who does not know christ.

Q   As a result of what you learned about the Great Commission/ Commandment above, how should this knowledge affect your personal testimony and evangelism practice?

It should push people to do the right thing knowing that Jesus will come again.

Q   How should it affect your involvement with new Christians?

It should provide you with the strength and confidence to spread the word.

Q   Thinking about your church's outreach and teaching programs, how could what you learned about the Great Commission/ Commandment above help strengthen these?

It should strengthen our outreach and open up christ to even more people.

Christians from non-Pentecostal traditions are often cautious, maybe even uneasy, when it comes to conversations about the Holy Spirit and the Spirit's empowerment. It feels safe to speak about the Holy Spirit as a part of the Trinity. Spiritual gifts are in these settings often explained as an enhancement of natural abilities. Pastors and church leaders will say, "It is important to find your spiritual gift because that will tell you where God wants you to serve in the church." In that scenario, the way to recognize which gift(s) God has given you is to determine what you truly enjoy and what you excel in doing. Once that is discovered, you need to train yourself even more in that area.

EPISODE 12 THIS GOSPEL SHALL BE FOR ALL PEOPLE

12

mc

ACT 1
A SOUND AS OF A RUSHING WIND
Acts 2–4, 10; Roman 8

There's much to be said for the understanding that God empowers people in relation to their personal makeup. Put differently, spiritual gifting is not disconnected from natural talent. God clearly gifts his people with different personalities and abilities. And to not use natural gifts for God's kingdom purposes would be senseless for a follower of Jesus. Furthermore, God's gifts are plainly working in cooperation with our personalities. The gift of evangelism, for example, can look very different from person to person. A Billy Graham stands up and speaks to masses of people—the gift of evangelism is evident when scores of people hear the gospel and respond by committing their lives to Jesus. Another person, without the ability to speak to large groups, can sit on a city bench and have a deep, significant, one-on-one conversation with a complete stranger—the gift of evangelism is evident when this conversation leads to the other person's surrender to the Lordship of Jesus Christ. It is the same gift, but it looks very different when given to two different personality types!

The above understanding of spiritual gifts is certainly helpful and true, but the Bible speaks also to an even deeper empowerment of the Spirit—an empowerment that goes beyond natural abilities and personality types. Without merely pointing to supernatural gifts, like healing, the book of Acts and the letters of Paul seem to reveal a pattern where the Spirit enables Christians to act in new ways that unquestionably point to God.

E12
A1

Martin Lloyd-Jones, the famed preacher from London's Westminster Chapel, quotes from John Wesley, Jonathan Edwards, and D. L. Moody, who explain their powerful encounters with the Holy Spirit:[*]

[John Wesley] Mr. Hall, Hinching, Ingham, Whitefield, Hutching, and my brother Charles were present at our love feast in Fetter Lane with about sixty of our brethren. About three in the morning as we were continuing instant in prayer the power of God came mightily upon us, insomuch that many cried out for exulting joy and many fell to the ground. As soon as we were recovered a little from the awe and amazement at the presence of His Majesty, we broke out with one voice, "We praise Thee O God, we acknowledge Thee to be the Lord."

[Jonathan Edwards] The Person of Christ appeared ineffably excellent with an excellency great enough to swallow up all thoughts and conceptions, which continued, as near as I can judge, about an hour; such as to keep me a greater part of the time in a flood of tears, and weeping aloud. I felt an ardency of soul to be, what I know not otherwise how to express, emptied and annihilated; to lie in the dust, and to be full of Christ alone; to love Him with a holy and pure love; to trust in Him; to live upon Him; to serve Him and to be perfectly sanctified and made pure, with a divine and heavenly purity.

[D. L. Moody] I kept on crying all the time that God would fill me with His Spirit. Well, one day in the City of New York—oh! What a day, I cannot describe it, I seldom refer to it. It is almost too sacred an experience to name. Paul had an experience of which he never spoke for fourteen years. I can only say, God revealed Himself to me, and I had such an experience of His love that I had to ask Him to stay His hand.

Step 1: Read the Story (Acts 2–4, 10; Romans 8)

Acts 2:1, 5

Q   Where were the disciples gathered when the Holy Spirit came?

At the temple

Acts 2:4; cf. 1:5

Q   How many of them were filled with the Holy Spirit?

11

---

[*] Martyn Lloyd-Jones, *Joy Unspeakable: Power and Renewal in the Holy Spirit* (Wheaton, IL: Harold Shaw, 1984), 62, 79–80.

Q Who was in Jerusalem for the celebration of Pentecost?   Acts 2:5–11

All of the believers and Peter.

Q When Peter preaches to the crowd in Acts 2:17–21, what prophetic text did he preach from?

The prophetic text from the Spirit, Psalm

Q Which two Psalms does he quote from in Acts 2:25–28 and
2:34–35?

Psalms 112 and Psalms 131

Q When the people were convicted by Peter's sermon, what did   Acts 2:37–39
he tell them to do to become part of the Christian community?

He told them to give up their old ways
and join with God.

Q Speaking of the community of the believers, what things does
Acts 2:42 highlight as first priorities of the church?

It highlighted that the church would
have many struggles.

Q What is the first healing miracle in the newly formed church?   Acts 3:1–10

The first miracle was the allowing
of the blind man to see.

Q Whom does Peter address in Acts 3:19, and what is the basis for
God's forgiveness of sin?

He talks of Adam and how his loyalty
would be shared with the people.

Q When Peter and John stand before the Sanhedrin, what do   Acts 4:12
they claim is the only way to salvation?

To become part of the church.

Acts 4:23–31

Q When the Sanhedrin release Peter and John, they tell them to not ever speak about Jesus again. What is the response of the church?

They retaliated and showed the widespread love for Jesus.

Acts 4:31

Q What happened when they finished their bold prayer?

When they finished the bold prayer they were in the presence of Christ.

Acts 6:1–6

Q How did the early church respond to the needs found among their members?

They did not give very much on their policies.

Q What does Romans 8:5–11 say about the mind that is controlled by the Spirit?

The mind that is controled will be the best mind.

Rom. 8:18–21

Q With what does Paul compare the suffering he is going through at the moment?

He compares it to the sufferings of the egypt people.

Q Related to prayer and intercession, what do we learn about the Spirit in Romans 8:26–34?

The best way to approach the Holy Spirit is through prayer.

Step 2: Find the Meaning of the Story

cf. TGS, pp. 316–18

Q The Jews gathered at Jerusalem for Pentecost. What did they celebrate?

They celebrated the ten commadments and 49 days after the Exodus of Egypt.

Q   Why do you think God sent his Holy Spirit during the cele-   cf. TGS, p. 318
bration of Pentecost? That is, how should that influence our
understanding of the Spirit's outpouring?

> God wanted to give back to the Jews
> who were doing what they were told.

Q   What changed in the disciples when you compare them right   cf. TGS, p. 318
before and after the outpouring of the Spirit?

> It changed there overall demenor from saddness
> of Jesus death to hopefullnes through the Spirit.

Q   When Luke tells the story of Jesus in his Gospel and about   cf. TGS, pp. 318–21
the early Christians in Acts, what parallels stand out the most
to you?

> It shows to me that the early Christians
> were ridiculd for what they were
> And who they praised.

Q   Often when we read a narrative section of Scripture we sub-   cf. TGS, pp. 321–23
consciously consider it mostly descriptive (history). In con-
trast, when we read a letter we read it as normative (theology).
Is such a distinction fair to the text? How would you explain
the relationship between history and theology (description
and normative)?

> Yes it is fair because It shows the effort that
> Paul put into the letters that he wrote. Description
> is more detailed specifics while normative is from
> a person who is writing.

Q   Give an example of an event in Acts that is not merely descriptive, but that Luke wrote down to show how things should be
in the church.

> The event that best speaks to me is that all
> of the Christians banded together for the church.

Q   Explain the word "repent."

Repent is trying to make up for something that you did wrong.

Q   If God convicts you to repent, what does that actually look like in your life? Explain not just your emotional response, but also the specifics of the situation.

It means that you should change your course in life to one that follows God.

Q   How would you explain the meaning of being filled with the Spirit, and why is it necessary?

Filled with the Spirit is full of grace and understanding to live a Godly life.

Q   Acts 2–4 tells of several Spirit-fillings of the same people. When do these occur?

These occur after the Pentecost

Q   How does this relate to your life as a Christian?

It makes me want to serve God.

Q   Acts follows a pattern of geographic expansion of the church. How does this relate to your personal calling as a witnessing disciple of Jesus?

It is an example that the church should always be expanding.

Preparing for the Next Act

Martyrdom—dying for one's testimony as a Christ-follower—is not something most people in the Western world know much about. Even the threat of it seems as something far removed in both time and geography to most westerners. Still, the word "Jesus" can create a strong opposition in many circles. It's okay to talk about God, but once Jesus enters the picture things can quickly change. Most people who are faithful witnesses to Christ can testify to some aspects of that.

ACT 2
THE CHURCH IN JERUSALEM AND THE EARLY SPREAD OF THE GOSPEL
Acts 5–12

One of the difficulties many Western Christians face is that they do not see much of a difference between their perspectives on life before and after they become followers of Christ. Many have come to equate a Western worldview with a Christian worldview. Being saved has more to do with the next world (the afterlife) than it has with participating in God's purposes for this world right now. Consequently, becoming a Christian does not often lead to a radical rethinking of one's approach to life or understanding of reality. Put differently, the narrative (or story) we follow as the guide to our understanding of life may not change much after we begin to consider the Christian faith a personal commitment. To illustrate, when you travel to other cultures you notice clear differences in thinking and lifestyle patterns. Their worldview is different! When someone becomes a Christian, his or her culture should change because new guidelines and new perspectives now rule the day (e.g., John 13:35; Phil. 2:3).

The early disciples experienced great persecution from the beginning because they "rewrote" their worldview. Acts 7 records the first public killing of a follower of Jesus. In what looks to most modern Christians as little more than a recounting of Israel's history, we get a picture of the consequences early Christians faced when they challenged the common worldview. Undeterred by what was unquestionably a most intimidating situation, Stephen, one of the first church deacons, boldly stood up in the midst of an angry crowd and explained God's purpose for his creation and the place God's people were supposed to assume in this purpose. Stephen retold God's story in a way that forced his listeners to rethink their understanding of reality. The crowd refused to do so and killed him instead.

E12
A2

Acts 5:1–2

Q   What did Ananias and Sapphira sell?

Fish

Acts 5:1–11

Q   What was the problem with their gift to the church?

It was not big enough

Acts 5:34–40

Q   What was Gamaliel's argument to the Sanhedrin that saved the disciples' life?

He said that killing of that man would do no good, just evil.

Acts 6:1–6;
cf. *TGS*, p. 326

Q   When church members carried their old culture or way of thinking into the church, the church elected seven deacons. What was the specific cause?

To keep the church on the right track

Acts 6:3

Q   What were the requirements for those elected to this position?

Men who had been members of the Church

Acts 7:44–50

Q   In Stephen's speech, what does he say about God's geographical limitation to the temple in Jerusalem?

He says that it should not expand too quickly.

Acts 8:9–23

Q   In Acts 8, Luke relates a story of a sorcerer who thought he could continue his old lifestyle while adding some power from the Holy Spirit. Why did Peter decline his request?

Giving him more power would take him further away from God.

Q One of Jesus' disciples, Philip, met with a prominent Ethiopian who asked to be baptized. What was Philip's requirement for doing that?

Acts 8:26–39;
cf. TGS, pp. 330–31

He had to repent and give all of the glory to God.

Q One of the most famous conversion stories in Christian history is recorded in Acts 9:1–22. Who was the person and what was the circumstance?

cf. TGS, pp. 326–27

Paul and God having a talk to make him repent and join the church.

Q Who introduced him to and convinced the church that he had become a trustworthy follower of Christ?

Acts 9:26

Stephen

Q When Peter came to Joppa he met a faithful disciple who became sick and died. Who was it, and what happened?

Acts 9:36–41

Thomas and because he turned away from the ways of Christ.

Q In Caesarea, Peter preached in the home of a Gentile. Before his visit to this home, God had to deal with Peter's worldview. What happened?

Acts 10:1–48
cf. TGS, p. 331

He had to change peter so that he would be more approachable.

Q While Peter spoke, the Holy Spirit fell on the Gentile listeners. What did Peter conclude after this?

Acts 10:44–47;
cf. 10:34–36

The Holy Spirit was upon them

| Acts 11:1–2 | Q | When Peter came back to Jerusalem, who was opposed to his meeting in Cornelius' house? | E12 A2 |

Saul

| Acts 11:19 | Q | Christians fled Jerusalem to avoid persecution. Where did they go? |

They fled to Israel

| Acts 11:26 | Q | Where were Jesus followers called Christians for the first time? |

Antioch

| Acts 13:1–3 | Q | Where was the church that sent out the first Christian missionaries located? |

Antioch

| | Q | Acts 12:12–17 explains how the early Christians met in homes for fellowship, prayer, and Bible study. In whose home did Peter meet with his group? |

They all met in Silas' howe

Step 2: Find the Meaning of the Story

| Acts 5:1–11 | Q | How does the story of Ananias and Sapphira relate to the tension between one's pre-Christian and Christian worldviews? |

It show how foolish the old life is compared to the rich awakening.

| Acts 6:1–6 | Q | How does the story of the election of the first deacons relate to struggles concerning one's change of thinking/behavior after conversion to Christ? |

It was a struggle with equality, but also with leadership.

Q   What was Stephen's most challenging point to get across to the   cf. Acts 6:13–14; 7:48–50

angry crowd? Beyond being told that they should have been more devoted to God, what truly made them angry?

The most challenging point was to prove that their old ways were wrong.

Q   How do you think Stephen's speech impacted Paul's thinking? How do you see it relate to his conversion in Acts 9?   Acts 8:54–58; cf. TGS, pp. 326–30

It impacted Paul in a way that no other line of thinking was right.

Q   In terms of Luke's presentation of the story, what connections do you think he saw between the Ethiopian and Cornelius, and how does that relate to God's kingdom purposes?   cf. TGS, pp. 330–32

They were two different, but the Lord brought them both to the same goal.

Q   Explain in your own words the significance of Peter's vision and how it relates to a necessary change of worldview for followers of Christ.

Peter's vision tells that people must change worldview to relate to God.

Q   List three major things that happened in Antioch that impacted the spread of the gospel forever.   cf. TGS, pp. 331–32

Christians, Spread, and transfer of like minded people.

E12
A2

Q Changing one's thinking and behavior is difficult. To be truly faithful to God's call for discipleship, what are some areas where your worldview needs to change?

Some changes would include turning more toward Christ.

Q If you were to apply the story of Simon the sorcerer to a contemporary situation, what would it be? How can the thinking that lies behind Simon's behavior be a warning to us not to think in similar ways in our modern contexts and situations?

People should not have more power to do bad things.

Q How would you explain the connection between worldview and culture?

Worldview is a mindset and culture is a way of life.

Q How does that connection relate to Christians and the culture of the Christian community (the church)?

The Church is the bride of Christ and his followers worship there.

Q Looking at the dynamic qualities of the newly started church in Antioch, how can you encourage your church to focus on the same passions?

Telling people to commit wholeheartedly to Christ.

Q How do you see the strong community between Peter and the church relate to the way you are engaged in community living in your church (or prayer/Bible study group)?

I live in a small community that is very much church centered.

Preparing for the Next Act

Travelling the globe to visit faraway places for the sake of missions has become a somewhat common experience for young American Christians. Short-term mission trips give many Western Christians a window into the situation of other Christians around the world, the setting where they serve and the difficulties they face. Mission travelers come back and are enthused about God's work. Long-term missionaries giving up careers, proximity to family, and other familiar things often come to experience a sense of relationship with the culture they serve for so long, that they work there almost as indigenous. Most active Christians, and evangelical Christians in particular, have always had a special love and appreciation for people who leave what they know to commit to a life of missions. All of the above is rooted in the Antiochian church's decision to send out Paul and Barnabas to start Christian communities around the world.

ACT 3
PAUL'S FIRST AND SECOND MISSIONARY JOURNEYS
Acts 13:1–18:22; Galatians

cf. *TGS*, pp. 329–30, chart "A Chronology of Paul's Life"; p. 336 map "The First Missionary Journey of Paul"; and p. 338 map "The Second Missionary Journey of Paul"

Paul's uncompromising steadfastness to start Christ-committed communities in all nations brought a unique awareness to Christian believers of all generations that God's message of redemption through Christ is intended for people from every tribe, language, people, and nation (Rev. 5:9). What Israel had missed by not heeding Isaiah's call to become a light unto the nations (Isa. 42:6–7), Paul saw as God's call to the church. Israel had missed their calling by focusing on their *position* as God's people. In contrast, Paul became the engine that drove to church to focus on their *purpose* as God's people. How can the nations hear unless someone preaches (Rom. 10:12–15)? The church's purpose as God's people is to be a light unto the nations. Christians cannot hide in provincial communities as if the gospel message was for their enjoyment alone. Rather, God aims to bring all his creation back to himself—to put an end to the consequences of the fall so to speak—and, he is using *his* people, the church, to announce redemption everywhere to everyone so that no one can say they have never heard. As Paul saw it, the church's call and election is for the *purpose* of being "God's messengers," not for the *status* of being "God's people." As Israel enjoyed exclusivity as God's special people *in the midst of* nations, Paul calls the church to recognize that they are God's empowered people *for the sake of* nations, so that they all may become God's people (1 Tim. 2:4–6).

Step 1: Read the Story (Acts 13:1–18:22; Galatians)

Acts 13:2   Q   When the church sent out its first two missionaries, who was mentioned first?

Peter

Acts 13:4   Q   Where did they go first?

Rome

Acts 13:5   Q   Whom did they bring?

Paul

Acts 13:13   Q   When and where did this person leave them again?

A few months later, Jerusalem

Acts 13:16–41   Q   Who did most of the preaching?

Peter

Q   In Acts 13:42, who is mentioned first (i.e., considered the leader)?

Paul

Q   Why did they move on to Lystra and Derbe?   Acts 14:1–7

Because they were close and needed help

Q   What was the first miracle in Lystra?   Acts 14:8–10

Helping the blind to see

Q   Which Greek gods do the people compare to Paul and Barnabas, respectively?   Acts 14:11–12

Zeus and Hermes

Q   After Paul was stoned and left for dead, what did the new Christians do? What was the setting and action that enabled Paul to get back up?   Acts 14:19–20

The new Christians started to help and were successful.

Q   Before returning to Antioch in Syria, Paul and Barnabas went back through the towns where they had seen people turn to Christ. How did they help encourage and establish communities in each of these towns?   Acts 14:21–25

They gave many speeches and preaches and help establish churches.

Q   What was the issue that resulted in the first council of the church?   Acts 15:1–5

Those that turned from God

E12
A3

Acts 15:12–29

Q What was the resolution? Summarize the content of the letter written to the newly started churches.

Turn to God. All of the problems of the world can be fixed by turning to God.

Acts 15:36–40

Q Whom did Paul bring on his second missionary journey?

Silas

Acts 15:36–40

Q Where did Barnabas go and whom did he bring?

Jerusalem and Silas

Acts 16:6–18:22

Q Where did Paul and Silas go on the second journey after visiting the churches Paul started on his first journey?

Athens

Acts 18:1

Q Where did Paul go after Athens?

Rome

Acts 18:2–3

Q What was the name of the couple with whom Paul worked as a tentmaker?

The Gentile Couple

Q Following traditional letter-writing style of the first century (cf. Gal. 1:1–5), Paul usually continues his letters with a thanksgiving section. But how does he begin Galatians?

He begins with a problem and how to fix it.

Gal. 2:11–13

Q As Paul rehearses his story, he reveals a confrontation he had with Peter. What was the issue?

Where to go?

Step 2: Find the Meaning of the Story

Q Paul and Barnabas began their journey to Barnabas' home-
town of Cyprus (Acts 4:36). Do you think Jesus' word from
Mark 5:19 may have had something to do with where they
started their journey? Explain.

That message spoke to them and told them were to go.

Q In Paul and Barnabas' two speeches to the people of Pisidian   Acts 13:14–48
Antioch, how do they connect Israel and the church as one
people sharing the same story and purpose?

Israel is the people of the God and Christians will soon be too.

Q The term "good news" (same Greek word we also translate
"gospel") is used several times in Acts 13–14. In which way is
the message of Paul and Barnabas good news to Jews? And in
which way is it good news to non-Jews?

Gospel is good news for everyone because it gives hope to everyone.

Q How would you explain the reaction of the Christians who   Acts 15:5; cf. TGS, p. 337
came from a Pharisaic background?

They would first dorp, but then realize the truth.

E12
A3

Acts 15:19–21, 29

Q   The church agreed not to put undue regulations on non-Jewish Christians. However, they did place some guidelines. Why these particular restrictions?

Restrictions need to be made to fulfill the Gospel.

Acts 16:11–15;
cf. *TGS*, pp. 337–42

Q   Who is the first convert we hear about in Europe?

Saul

cf. *TGS*, p. 339

Q   Why do you think Luke spends this much time on Lydia and mentions more than once that she has a home and a household of servants?

He thought that it needed more time for people.

Acts 12:5–7

Q   Paul and Silas were in prison and, as happened in other situations, Luke explains how their worship in prison (Acts 16:16–40) led to their freedom (cf. Acts 12:5–7). Why do you think Luke highlights these connections (i.e., difficulties leading to freedom)?

It shows signs of struggle and how god will help you through.

Acts 17:16–34;
cf. *TGS*, pp. 340–41

Q   Explain in your own words Paul's approach to preaching the gospel in Athens. How does he connect with his audience?

He preaches in a way that they would understand.

cf. *TGS*, pp. 341–43

Q   We often think that the only thing that directed Paul's itinerary were specific revelations from God (e.g., Acts 16:9–10).

However, other factors may have played a role as well. What enabled Paul to stay for 18 months in Corinth?

He had friends and other that helped him.

Step 3: Make the Story Your Own

Q   How would you define the word "missionary"?

travel to spread the word

Q   Do you see yourself as a missionary? Why or why not?

Yes, because in all my travels I show the gospel.

Q   How does the beginning point of Paul's first missionary journey speak to your beginning point as a missionary?

It shows that we both had a purpose to spread at that time.

Q   If you were to find a couple of modern parallels to Acts 15:5, what would they be?

They would be the people of the Church going all over to spread the word.

Q   Can you think of anything you need to think differently about in your own heart after reflecting on Acts 15:5?

No not really, very similar

E12
A3

Q   What is the strength of Paul's approach to preaching in Athens, and what can you learn from that as you speak to people about Jesus today?

It shows how much strength one can get in the face of adversity.

Q   We don't know if a church was established in Athens, but Paul had established a thriving church in Corinth. What can you learn from 1 Corinthians 2:2 as you share your faith?

You do the best you can but not everything is going to work out like you want it to.

Preparing for the Next Act

There is something uniquely captivating about people who are driven by a single vision. Think of athletes training for the Olympics, for example, how they subordinate everything else to this one focus. They go to bed when others stay up late to watch a movie, and get up early to exercise when others are sleeping. Eating patterns, and the very food they eat, are changed to best benefit their athletic purposes. When others relax, they exercise; when others go on vacation, they go to training camps; when others celebrate special events with nice dinners and dessert, they abstain from indulging. They have one focus, one goal under which everything else is subordinated! Other things may be important and pleasant, but these are only "given room" to the degree they do not hinder reaching the athletic goal. Discipline and self-control are required for one whose eyes are on the victory stand.

ACT 4
PAUL'S THIRD MISSIONARY JOURNEY, ARREST, AND FINAL DAYS
Acts 18:23–28:30; Ephesians

The dynamic quality of Paul's character came from his having such a laser-sharp focus on God's purposes for his creation. After being almost stoned to death, Paul got up and went right back into the city (Acts 14:19–20); when in prison, he praised God (Acts 16:25); fleeing for his life from one city, he went directly to the next to preach the same gospel (Acts 17:10); when facing danger from the crowd in a riot, he still wanted to stand up to get a hearing for his message (Acts 19:31). Realizing it might cost him his life to go back into Jerusalem, he didn't dwell on his own fears, but used his farewell speech to encourage church elders to stay the course. Summing up his singular and vibrant focus, he said: "I consider my life worth nothing to me, if only I may finish the race and complete the task the Lord Jesus has given me—the task of testifying to the gospel of God's grace" (see Acts 20:17–35).

Paul used his third journey to raise money among the Gentile churches for the poverty-stricken church in Jerusalem. When he got there, instead of being celebrated, he was taken captive and imprisoned in the harbor town of Caesarea. When he as a Roman citizen prisoner came to stand before the Roman governor, Felix, he used the opportunity to try to lead Felix to faith. When Felix was replaced as a governor, Paul used his citizenship rights to request a hearing before the emperor in Rome. Did Paul hope for the conversion of Caesar himself? It's likely! To his last breath, Paul trusted that if he would be faithful in sharing the gospel, God's kingdom purposes would find fulfillment and Christ would return to restore all things to himself.

cf. *TGS*, p. 353 chart "Getting a Grip on the Sequence of Acts"

Step 1: Read the Story (Acts 18:23–28:30; Ephesians)

Q In Ephesus, where did Paul go when the synagogue did not welcome him?

Acts 19:8–10

He went to Jail

Q Itinerant preachers may have been great communicators with great insight, but some still needed guidance from mature Christians. Who guided Apollos?

Acts 18:24–26

Paul and Silas

Q The firmest historical evidence we have for dating Paul's journeys is found in Acts 18:12. Who was the proconsul of Achaia at that time?

It was the person that appeared before.

Q Where did Paul go after Corinth?

Acts 19:1

Rome

Acts 19:23–41

Q   As large numbers of people came to faith in Ephesus, business people paid attention. Explain in your own words what happened.

When large amount of people Start doing something People Notice and want to do.

Acts 20:1–6

Q   Where did Paul go after Ephesus?

Rome

Acts 20:7–12

Q   What happened in Troas and how does that relate to Acts 9:36–41?

The people did not listen and so they had to move on.

Acts 20:17

Q   From the harbor city of Miletus, whom did Paul send for?

Barnabas

Acts 20:32

Q   To whom did Paul commit the church in Ephesus when he left?

Peter

Acts 21:8–11

Q   While Paul was visiting Philip in Caesarea, he learned of the destiny that would be his if he went to Jerusalem. How did he find out?

He found out because someone spilled the beans.

Acts 21:27–29

Q   What was the argument the Jews used to get public opinion turned against Paul?

They said that Paul had been like him and nothing happened.

Acts 23:6–8

Q   What did Paul say to create a stir in the Sanhedrin between the Sadducees and the Pharisees?

He said that the other were inferior to the other.

Q   What was the direct reason Paul got transferred from Jerusalem to Caesarea? *Acts 23:12–22*

The people needed him there so he went.

Q   What was the name of the governor who followed Felix in Caesarea? *Acts 24:27*

Deraphonia

Q   As a prisoner in Caesarea, Paul had a chance to defend himself before the grandson of Herod the Great who ruled when Jesus was born. What was this king's name? *Acts 25:13*

Perophthmiea

Q   What was that grandson's response to the message about the person his grandfather tried to kill? *Acts 26:28–32*

He dissagreed and so paul did not get killed.

Q   On what island did Paul shipwreck on his way to Rome? *Acts 28:1*

Easter Islad

Q   What event changed the islanders' opinion of Paul? *Acts 28:2–10*

When all of the people survied on the ship through the bad storm.

Q   When Paul came to Rome, how did he approach the Jewish population? *Acts 28:17–22*

He approached them with caution knowing their importance.

E12
A4

163

cf. *TGS*, pp. 345–46

Q   Why did Priscilla and Aquila pull Apollos aside to teach him more about the way of the Lord, when Acts 18:24 says he was a learned man with a thorough knowledge of Scripture?

They knew that he needed more attention then the rest.

Q   Compare Acts 18:7 and 19:8–9. From this reading, how would you summarize Paul's approach to evangelism when he entered a new city?

He approached with caution and then told the news.

Q   Compare 1 Corinthians 16:3 and Acts 18:27. Why do you think it was important for Christians to bring a letter of recommendation regarding their faithfulness as believers when they wanted to join a new church in a new place?

It showed that the people could actually commit to what they needed to do.

Acts 24:17; 1 Cor. 16:2–4;
2 Cor. 8–9;
Rom. 15:25–27
cf. *TGS*, pp. 347–48

Q   Paul used his third missionary journey to raise money among Gentile churches for the poor church in Jerusalem. Do you think Paul may have done this to try to create a stronger bond of community between Gentile and Jewish Christians?

Yes he wanted a stronger bond

Acts 24:9–21; 26:1–29

Q   Explain in your own words how Paul used his opportunity to defend himself before the Roman authorities.

He threw out all that he had done in hope they would understood.

Q What is the significance of Paul's approach toward the Jewish population when he came to Rome? What does this tell us about Paul's focus on accomplishing God's purposes?

He approached people with unlike minds to bring them together.

Step 3: Make the Story Your Own

Q If you have been a Christian for a while, what can you learn from Priscilla and Aquila?

cf. Acts 18:24–26

Yes I can learn from these two to help.

Q What can you learn from Pricilla and Aquila's use of their home?

That one should open up all door to help Christians.

Q How do you think the early Christians' use of recommendation letters relates to transfer of membership between churches today? Or, what could we learn from that approach?

cf. Acts 18:27

There needs to be more community in the church and this would help.

Q Paul's collection shows that he wanted churches and Christians to consider each other family regardless of distance (Corinth was in every way unrelated to Jerusalem). How could your church support a poor, struggling church in a different state?

We have sent money to other churches when Hurricane Katrina went through.

E12
A4

Q   When Paul has an opportunity to defend himself against accusations, he preaches the gospel instead. Can you think of a personal situation where you, instead of defending yourself, shared your faith? Explain.

I did that when I was being bullied and to act good to all neibors.

Q   Being angry with (or fearful of) a certain people group whom you feel has caused you pain or grief is not uncommon. What can you learn from Paul's big-hearted approach in Acts 28:17–20?

Instead of fearing for then One should pray for them.

Preparing for the Next Act

When we say it's hard to teach an old dog new tricks, what we mean is that habits can be hard to break. People get set in their ways. This is true in a lot of areas of life. The word *culture* captures what may be considered the common habits of a certain population or group of people. Moreover, culture and/or habits are usually grounded in a certain way of thinking—the collected thinking of a group over time. People usually decide when to eat and how long to sit at the table, what to celebrate and how to celebrate it, what is considered polite and impolite, etc., based on patterns learned over a lifetime.

Many of these patterns or habits have religious roots even when those who are adhering to them have no idea why they are doing things the way they are. "It's just habit—it's how we've always done it." People unfamiliar with habits they find unusual or odd may simply brush off the differences with a simple different-strokes-for-different-folks remark.

EPISODE 13 CHURCH GROWTH AND CHURCH STRUGGLES

13

MC

ACT 1
CHURCH STRUGGLES AND THE EXAMPLES FROM 1 CORINTHIANS
1 Corinthians 3–7; 11–14

This issue of ingrained habits was part of what Paul was up against when he shared the gospel in a setting where people had zero understanding of the stories, thinking, and habits of the Jewish people and the biblical narrative. It is one thing to preach the gospel to a group who knows the stories of the patriarchs and the prophets and who live in the expectation of a coming Messiah sent from God. It is quite a different thing to minister to converts from cultures where nothing from the biblical narrative makes sense in light of the way they grew up. When Paul preached the gospel in Corinth, the Corinthians who became followers of Christ were faced with questions about their lifestyle and ethics that required a complete rethinking of their habits and priorities. The gospel could not find a springboard from which it could jump like it would in Jerusalem. Rather, the narrative of their pagan stories led them away from God. God's story challenged them to rethink everything they'd known.

Paul's letters, especially 1 Corinthians, are evidence of the struggles faced by new Christians in pagan settings. Because Paul addresses specific and practical questions head on, these letters function both as a powerful testimony to the struggles of the early church and as a worthy guide to the questions and lifestyle patterns of the modern church.

Step 1: Read the Story (1 Corinthians 3–7; 11–14)

Q   How does Paul help the church overcome their "favorite preacher" divisions?

1 Cor. 3:1–7; cf. *TGS*, p. 359

He lets the gospel pick it.

cf. *TGS*, pp. 359–60

Q What is the issue related to immorality that Paul discusses in 1 Corinthians 5?

It states that people had no respect for christ.

Q In 1 Corinthians 5:9–11, Paul deals with judgment. He seems to make a distinction between two groups. How does he distinguish them?

He prayed to God and it revealed who they were.

cf. *TGS*, p. 360

Q In 1 Corinthians 7, what is Paul's preference regarding marriage? Why is he still recommending it for many?

Between one man and one woman because God wanted it that way.

cf. *TGS*, p. 361

Q In your own words, explain Paul's argument in 1 Corinthians 8 related to Christians eating meat?

He stated that eating meat was wrong but no where in the scriptures is this so.

1 Cor. 11:3–16; cf. *TGS*, p. 362 for pictures of head coverings in the first century

Q In terms of head covering, which gender does Paul address first?

Female

cf. *TGS*, pp. 361–63

Q What does he say about head covering and men related to worship?

They should wear only outside on the days.

cf. *TGS*, pp. 361–63

Q What does he say about head covering and women related to worship?

They should wear them in the church to identify them.

Q   What metaphor does Paul use to explain how spiritual gifts work together?

1 Cor. 12

The blind hog finds an acorn

Q   What does he say about prominence in the church and spiritual gifting?

cf. TGS, p. 363

The more people in the church, the more spiritual Gifts seen.

Step 2: Find the Meaning of the Story

Q   Since the pronouns are plural in 1 Corinthians 3:16–17, what is Paul referring to when he talks about God's temple?

The many Churches and people.

Q   How does 1 Corinthians 3:17 relate to the discussion on division in the church? How does God view those who create divisions?

cf. TGS, p. 359

Those who create divisions are to be punished.

Q   The sin described in 1 Corinthians 5 seems so grievous that it is almost incomprehensible that the Corinthian church could allow this to occur. What do you think caused them to allow this kind of behavior in their midst?

cf. TGS, pp. 359–60

The people had little to no control over what others did.

Q   Rephrase in your own words Paul's teaching regarding remarriage in 1 Corinthians 7:8–16.

One should not break the bondage of marriage the first time.

Q   Who are the strong Christians, and who are the weak Christians?

1 Cor. 8:7–8; cf. TGS, p. 361

The Jews were strong, the gentiles not so much

E13
A1

1 Cor. 11:3–16   **Q**   Why did Paul care about head coverings related to worship?

The Lord sayed that it was important so Paul helped.

cf. *TGS*, pp. 361–63   **Q**   What was the issue with men and women, respectively, regarding head coverings?

The issue was each gender role with the church.

1 Cor. 12; cf. *TGS*, p. 363   **Q**   Explain why Paul's body metaphor is so helpful for how spiritual gifts relate to each other.

It is an easy way for people to connect and spread the word.

Step 3: Make the Story Your Own

Q   How would you help people focus on the church community rather than on personal preferences for how things are done in church?

Help others know that even out of Church God is important.

Q   Regarding church discipline:

1.   How can self-righteousness be avoided among those who charge others of sin?

One must look closely at themselves first before judging others.

2.   What would be a proper and loving approach for you as a church member to use related to church discipline?

Approach people with an open mind instead of hate.

Q   Regardless of Paul's clear teaching, singleness is often less
    appreciated than married life by those in the church. What can
    a church do to change that?

It can encourage often to think
of the advantages of marrige instead
of disadvantaes.

Q   Standing up for one's personal rights has almost become a cor-
    nerstone for modern Western thinking about freedom. Paul
    asks us not to claim our rights for the sake of other (weaker)
    Christians. Consider some practical examples of how this
    applies to your life.

We should not hold ourselues up on
pedestals, rather hold God up.

Q   Paul's discussion of head covering related to worship ultimately
    has to do with distinguishing Christian worship from pagan
    worship and private entertainment events. Can you think of a
    parallel situation in the modern Western world where Chris-
    tian worship could be confused with a secular event? What
    kind of advice would Paul need to give today to help Chris-
    tians make a clear distinction between their Christian worship
    and popular/secular worship?

Christain worship is for the church ad secular
is for good acts, but not in the presence of
the congregation.

Seeking prominence in the church can still be a problem today. List a couple of prominent positions in the church and a couple of inconspicuous positions. Then consider how you can help the church and individual church members give more prominence to the inconspicuous.

The church should have a preacher and deacons not this worship leader crap that is not in the bible.

Preparing for the Next Act

"Think before you act," we say. Mostly, that statement is meant as an encouragement for people to avoid mindlessly starting something that is clearly foolish and will bear no good fruit. It is usually meant as a comment designed to discourage knee-jerk reactions.

ACT 2
CHURCH STRUGGLES AND CHRISTIAN THINKING
Colossians; 1 Timothy; Philemon; 1 John

Related to Paul's encounter with cultures foreign and completely alien to the gospel message, however, the statement "think before you act" is not a warning against knee-jerk reactions, but a truism. Thinking (even if subconscious) should always go before action. Thinking is the basis of aspirations, hopes, morality, and ultimately, therefore, action. As mentioned in the previous chapter, culture is the behavior of a group of people that results from the collective thinking of that group over time.

Many of the struggles Paul and the early Christians faced when spreading the gospel message to new nations, languages, and cultures were created by the clashes between the thoughts and philosophies of these regions and the biblical narrative. The new thinking that ensued from God's revelation of himself in Jesus Christ pointed in a completely different direction that their old way of thinking. In many ways, the greatest challenge the early church faced was to help the new Christians change their patterns of thinking (or worldview) to align with biblical thinking about God and neighbor. In that regard, they were up against enormous odds. They were faced with changing the thinking and behavior of generations of family traditions, and helping new Christians find a way to hold their own when everyone around them was affirming traditions and thought-patterns that ran contrary to the gospel message.

Step 1: Read the Story (Colossians; 1 Timothy; Philemon; 1 John)

Q   The book of Philemon deals with a major social issue in the first-century Roman world—a slave (Onesimus) and a slave owner (Philemon) who both became Christians. What did Paul say happened to their relationship?

cf. TGS, pp. 367–68

They all have common ground that each can relate to, find that.

Q   Philosophical and religious pluralism, where people "cut and paste" from a variety of sources and philosophies to create their own truth, was just as alive then as it is now.

cf. TGS, p. 369 sidebar "Pluralism"

1. How does Paul address the question of the sufficiency of Christ alone?

Col. 1:15–23

Paul is wrong in questioning the words and works of God.

2. What does Paul say about thought patterns that are rooted in human tradition?

Col. 2:4–10

Humans think of themselves as better which is not good.

3. What does Paul say about those who claim to have special knowledge and insight that is not readily available to all?

Col. 2:18

He says that there are special gifts from God that should be used for good.

cf. *TGS*, pp. 372–73

Q Gnosticism, with its strong claim of a separation between body and soul (matter and spirit), seemed attractive to many new Christians.

1 John 2:3–6

1. What does John say about love for God and obedience to God?

He says that it should be displayed in everything that we do.

1 John 2:9–11

2. How does John connect inner conviction to outer behavior?

He says that they should come together as one for good.

1 John 4:2–3

3. What does John say about those who separate the spirit of Christ from the body of Jesus?

He says that they have the wrong mindset to come out.

Step 2: Find the Meaning of the Story

cf. *TGS*, p. 367 sidebar "The Structure of Paul's Argumentation"

Q Explain what is meant by the indicative/imperative approach to teaching, and give an example from Paul's letters.

Indicative is a casual approach and imperative mean that it is crucial to know.

Q What needed to change in Philemon's thinking, and what did Paul tell him to do?

He needed to think more as a follower of God rather than one of the few to teach it.

Q   What needed to change in Onesimus' thinking, and what did Paul tell him to do?

He needed to think of his life as a service to God not to a man.

Q   Explain the difference between social pluralism (a good thing)   cf. *TGS*, pp. 369–70 and philosophical/religious pluralism (a bad thing).

Social is doing good things to show to others while religious is taking oneself for granted.

Q   What is the danger in claiming that a private experience gives special spiritual authority?

God meant for people to share the Gospel, not for someone to hold it in.

Q   How does Colossians 3:12–17 relate to the discussion on division in the church? How does God view those who create divisions?

He says that division in the church is not good for the whole congregation.

Q   How would you distinguish between genuine humility and false humility?

Genuine humility has feeling rather than false no feeling.

Q   Explain Gnosticism in your own words.   cf. *TGS*, pp. 372–73

Staying selfish with godly acts instead of sharing in the gospel with others.

E13
A2

Q   Why did John and the early Christians consider it such a danger?

It was a force that could pull the members of the church apart.

Step 3: Make the Story Your Own

Q   Think of a behavioral pattern to which you would like to speak a word of correction. What is it, and what biblical event would you use as the basis for your argument (indicative) and how would you argue for an action from it (imperative)?

One behavioral pattern that needs to change is christains not helping each other through struggles.

Q   What criteria would you use to discern when an argument that sounds persuasive is actually false in relation to the biblical message?

It would be based on history and the godliness of the person being refered to.

Q   An appeal to things you grew up thinking were right can be very persuasive on an emotional level and can often move a whole crowd, even when it is contrary to biblical teaching. What can you do to avoid being pulled into this type of persuasion?

To prevent this one should show true humility to those that oppose the christian walk.

Q   Separating one's spiritual life from one's real life and daily decision making is an easy temptation to fall into. What are some steps you can take to help avoid a separation of body and spirit in your Christian life?

Many times one could pray and think of spiritual things to remind of God glory.

Q   What steps can you take that will help you and other Christians to align your thinking more and more with Christ's teaching, so that it may bring about a change in your priorities and actions?

Christian should lean to band together to get across to those with other feelings.

Q   Heresy is claiming that false teaching is true. Hypocrisy is claiming godly actions without actually doing them. Many people are quick to use the word *heresy* when people disagree with them. Jesus used the word *hypocrisy* when people's actions did not correspond to their words. Applying the meaning of these two words, in what way is a separation of spirituality and action an expression of heresy? In what way is it hypocrisy?

It is heresy when people do not turn to God or teach falsely. Hypocracy is when they do not act like how they sound.

The connection between faith, action, and salvation has led to fierce discussions among Christians. Can you have faith without actions that prove the reality of your faith? Are actions needed for salvation? Are specific actions necessary for salvation? What is faith anyway? Can faith be explained as conviction or mental assent? Or is faith the active behavior that expresses convictions about God whether such convictions can be articulated clearly or not? Is the ability to verbally confess specific beliefs about Christ the hinge upon which the door of eternal salvation hangs? If to have faith in someone is to trust them, how does trust relate to behavior or action? What does "trust" mean without action?

ACT 3
CHURCH STRUGGLES AND ISSUES OF FAITH
Hebrews 1–5; 9–10; James 2; Galatians 2:11–21; 1. Timothy 3:1–7; Titus 1:5–9

If people are saved by grace through faith (Eph. 2:8), how does grace relate to faith? Does grace cause faith? Does faith cause grace? Or, are they not causally related at all? What is grace anyway? Is grace a mere synonym for getting a second and third chance? Is grace a Christian code word for saying that humans play no real role in the question of salvation? Or, is grace the Christian term for God opening a door that humans could not open, but must go through now that God has opened it? Is grace what grandma and grandpa show when after a whole day in the park where you have misbehaved, you get the ice cream anyway? Is grace God's gift to humans that then calls for human faith (or trust/loyalty) as their gift to God in return?

Questions like these and their answers have puzzled people for generations and have caused significant debates—even rifts—between Christians. Paul clearly rejected his earlier pharisaic idea that eternal salvation could be found simply by getting circumcised and adhering to certain laws. For Paul, the forgiveness necessary to nullify the eternal consequences for human sin was found in Christ, not in circumcision and the law.

Many of the questions above likely would have mystified Paul and the other New Testament authors. For example, the division between *old* and *new* testaments is foreign to the authors of Scripture who saw the new testament as fulfillment of the old rather than as a correction of something different. The story of God begins in Genesis and ends in Revelation. It's a story about God's relationship with his creation and about his plan to restore unto himself what was broken through human rebellion.

Step 1: Read the Story (Hebrews 1–5; 9–10; James 2; Galatians 2:11–21; 1 Timothy 3:1–7; Titus 1:5–9)

Q How does Hebrews 1 explain the role of Christ in God's plan for his creation?

It explains that God knew of the fall and designed Christ to save the people.

Q How does Hebrews 3 explain the relationship between Christ and Moses?

They both started new covenants but Christs was everlasting.

Q How does Hebrews 4 explain the relationship between Christ and Joshua?

Joshua and Christ were alike because they both followed Gods orders.

Q How do Hebrews 5 and 9 explain the relationship between Christ and the High Priest?

Christ and the high priest were alike in that they led a charge to worship God.

Q How does Hebrews 10 explain the relationship between faith and salvation?

Faith is the believing in something and salvation is what is rewarded for positive faith.

E13
A3

Q   How does James 2 explain the relationship between faith, action, and salvation?

All of these are a process and that doing works in one catagory affects the others.

Q   How does Galatians 2:11–21 explain the relationship between faith, works of Law, and salvation?

It showed that each of these was important, but together they all help the body of Christ.

Step 2: Find the Meaning of the Story

cf. *TGS*, pp. 375–76

Q   Hebrews is an apologetics letter (or sermon) designed to help Jews who had become Christians and who were now under pressure from their families and friends to revert back to Judaism. How would you summarize Hebrews' argument?

The people need to see that Christ is the way to go and no other way can satify.

e.g., Gal. 2:16;
cf. *TGS*, pp. 376–78

Q   What does Paul mean by the phrase "works of Law"?

He means works that are helping or pertain to the Law of the Lord.

James 2:14–26

Q   What does James mean by the word "works"?

He means how a person carries out tasks in their daily life.

180

Q   Are the two expressions mutually exclusive (disagreement between Paul and James) or can they both be true at the same time? Explain.

I think that they both have their truths at some time or another.

Q   One of the big issues the early church faced was the selection of leadership. What are the three areas of qualification Paul spells out?

1 Tim. 3:1–7;
Titus 1:5–9;
cf. TGS, pp. 378–79

Strong faith, good works, relationship to others.

Q   What specific gift is included in Paul's list as a qualification?

cf. TGS, p. 379; p. 380 chart "Overseer/Elder Qualifications"

Salvation

Step 3: Make the Story Your Own

Q   In your own life, what pressures are you under (from family, friends, or others) to go easy on your Christian convictions and not upset their perspectives on life?

I am pressured by God, my family, and my congregation to uphold Christian convictions.

E13
A3

Q   Related to what you wrote above regarding the relationship between Galatians 2 and James 2 (faith and actions), how would
you explain this issue to a non-Christian who asks you what
it means to be saved by grace and what difference that should
make in his or her behavior?

A non Christian has nothing to look forward to in death and revealing to then Christ is the best action to be saved.

Q   Also related to what you wrote above regarding the relationship between Galatians 2 and James 2 (faith and actions), how
would you explain this issue to new Christians who says that
since they are saved by grace and have Jesus in their hearts,
their lifestyle ultimately makes no difference?

It is true that acts have no baring on whether one is saved or not, but it should be a goal to live more like Christ.

Q   The criteria for leadership in 1 Timothy all point to maturity.
Pick one from each of the three categories and explain in a
practical way how others would be able to recognize each in an
individual leader. For example, how would you know if someone is "temperate/self-controlled" or "a lover of goodness"?

A person that exibits self control would understand others situation and not get frustrated with bad thoughts.

Preparing for the Next Act

Most parents consider providing for their children a sacred trust. Good parents care both for their children's present and future. Regarding the word *provide*, most people think of making sure that the necessary resources, or means of support, are and will be available. An employer, for example, who provides for his or her employees, makes sure they have a good salary and a decent retirement plan. Bringing *provisions* on a trip usually refers to the food and equipment necessary to make the trip a success.

The word *providence* is closely related to this. Because this term usually includes the notion of foresight, or knowing what will be necessary in the future, many people connect this term with God—God's foreseeing care and guidance for his creation. To affirm God's providence is to affirm that history is not merely a haphazard flow of meaningless events, that sin is not omnipotent, and that God's story is moving toward its final goal. God has provided eternally for his people.

E13
A3

EPISODE 14 LOOKING FOR A CITY

14

(MC)

ACT 1
GOD'S FUTURE FOR HIS PEOPLE
Mark 13; Revelation 1–5; 18–19

The book of Revelation was written to Christians under severe persecution. Christians who, because of the cruelty they faced due to their faith, rightly could ask whether God was truly in charge of world history. To those who were thrown before wild animals to be eaten alive just because they confessed that Jesus, rather than Emperor Domitian, was Lord, it could easily look like the Emperor and the mighty empire of Rome had the upper hand. The message that God's kingdom has already come, albeit not in full, seemed to be contradicted by every experience they had. The message that God would let those who were faithful and trusting in him prosper and live long in the land, seemed more like wishful thinking than a statement related to reality.

To help give people hope and see further than their immediate experience of pain and suffering, God gave the apostle John a vision of hope to share with the Christians: God is still in charge and has not forgotten about his people. No emperor on earth and no power in the universe will be able to thwart God's plan or confuse the ending to God's story.

Step 1: Read the Story (Mark 13; Revelation 1–5; 18–19)

Q   In Mark 13, what are three signs Jesus mentions as the beginning of the end?

Lots of prayer, rejoicing from believers, and the appearance of Jesus.

Q   What are two of the illustrations Jesus uses to highlight the suddenness of the end-time events?   Mark 13:14–16

The appocolypse with fire and the quickness to be with him.

Q   In Revelation 2–3, which church does not get any praise?

Muslim and non believers

Q   List one praise and one correction for three of the churches listed in Revelation 2–3.

They are all praised for being followers of God, but are corrected in the ways.

Q   What are the ways or position of worship of those before the throne of God?   Rev. 4–5

Those that are before the throne shall act richeously and fully him.

Q   Compare and contrast the song about God and the song about Babylon.   Rev. 4:8; Rev. 18:10

The song about God is praising him. And the song of Babylon is of the fall.

Q   What kind of banquet are people invited to in Revelation 19:9–10?

banquet of believers with the lord.

Q   How does Revelation 19:19–21 describe the fate of those who have worshiped the beast?

It states that those shall not live in heaven with those that do good faith.

E14
A1

Q   In literature, *genre* is the style in which something is written. Genre speaks both to meaning and possible interpretation. Poetry, for example, reads much differently than a law text and does not carry the same rules for interpretation. Revelation is written in the genre of apocalypticism. After consulting TGS, pp. 388–90, or a book on biblical interpretation, explain this genre in your own words.

Revelation, much like Daniell is written in Apocolyptic writing.

Q   Noting that Mark 13 uses the apocalyptic genre, what is the historical meaning behind the symbols?

The Symbols stand for a higher Power.

Q   How would you explain the difference in genre between Revelation 1–3 and the rest of Revelation?

One shows signes of hope and the other is a prediction on the end.

Q   Revelation is a prophetic book. Biblical prophecy usually has a near view/far view structure (forthtelling/foretelling). Looking back to Episode 6, how would you explain this structure as it relates to the book of Revelation?

I would say the view is both rear and fear depending on how one looks at it.

Q   The book of Revelation was written to persecuted Christians who realized a gruesome death might be their next experience. How does Revelation bring hope to those enduring suffering?

It talks of those who strugle but will find hope through Christ.

Q   What does it mean to call someone Lord when it is not just a
     title?

It means that they have the most power over all people.

Step 3: Make the Story Your Own

Q   Give an example from your own Bible reading where you
     could have misread a text if you had not paid attention
     to genre.

The plagues to me were a bad thing if not looked at in the right Genere.

Q   Christians often interpret reality from their own experiences.
     When things go well around them they don't sense that the
     end is near. When things around them are inexplicably evil or
     devastating, they tend to be more alarmed. However, the expe-
     rience of "God is in control" for a wealthy American Christian
     may differ vastly from the experience of a hungry, persecuted
     Christian shunned from her surroundings. How can you avoid
     letting your immediate situation drive the urgency of your
     testimony and faith commitment?

Knowing how to stay calm in bad situations and taking time to remember the Lord is the best way.

Q   What practical steps can you take in your personal life
     that help you to never lose sight of God's providential care
     and guidance?

I can remember him in all that I do and take the time to not move too quickly.

E14
A1

Q   Hope gives energy and strength for life. Write a *practical* paragraph on living under the impact of hope.

Hope gives a Christian something to look forward to in bad times.

Q   In your daily life, what does it mean for you that Jesus is Lord? What do you do differently because of it?

Because Jesus is Lord, I know that he will always care for me.

Preparing for the Next Act

Most westerners do not think much about the symbolic value of numbers. In fact, unless we are talking about a price for an item, a size of a dress, or the age of a person, numbers are just that—numbers! In other cultures, and especially in ancient cultures, numbers carry meaning. Deeper realities or meanings are expressed when circumstances or events fit certain number values.

Take the number four, for example. To mention just a few examples, in Buddhism there are four noble truths and four great elements (earth, water, fire, wind); in Hinduism there are four stages of life and four strata of society (castes); in Islam there are four archangels and four sacred months of the year; in Judaism God's name is a tetragram (four letters: YHWH), there are four cups to drink at Passover and four expressions of redemption to be recited. Christianity has four Gospels and the book of Revelation has four horsemen. The number four likewise plays a special role in math, science, philosophy, technology, and even sports. Numbers other than four could demonstrate this point equally well.

ACT 2
GOD BRINGS HIS STORY TO ITS CLIMACTIC END
Matthew 24; 1 Thessalonians 4; 2 Thessalonians 2; Revelation 20–22

The Bible makes frequent use of certain numbers that clearly carry meaning beyond the countable. Think, for example, of the number twelve (Israel's number of tribes), or seven (the number of holiness), or ten (the number of perfection). Many of these numbers occur not only by themselves but as multiplied numbers. Solomon began building the temple exactly twelve generations (a generation is forty years) after the exodus from Egypt (1 Kings 6:1—forty years times twelve). Jesus sends out seventy disciples (seven times ten).

So should the numbers in the book of Revelation be read as mere numbers to be counted, or are they primarily symbolic in nature—that is, are they used to give reference to a deeper reality which is best expressed by numbers? Symbolic use of numbers is prevalent in apocalyptic literature, and this is evident in Revelation as well. The number for holiness, seven, is used repeatedly. Seven minus one (6), repeated three times, becomes the number of antichrist (666). The number ten, representing perfection, lifted to the third power (one thousand), holds a central place. Israel's number, twelve, multiplied by itself and then by one thousand (144,000) refers to a special group of people, and so on.

How one understands the significance of all these numbers will determine one's reading of Revelation—especially end-time texts like Revelation 20. Does the thousand-year reign, the millennium, refer to a literal one thousand years or to a perfect time period (ten to the power of three) set aside by God?

Christians throughout history have generally held one of three major millennial views—amillennialism, historic premillennialism, and postmillennialism. A fourth view, dispensational premillennialism, or dispensationalism, gained prominence primarily in the United States during the twentieth century.

Consult a Bible dictionary or *TGS*, pp. 393–400 for a short, clear overview of these various perspectives.

cf. *TGS*, pp. 394–400 for charts on the four millennial views

Step 1: Read the Story (Matthew 24; 1 Thessalonians 4; 2 Thessalonians 2; Revelation 20–22)

Q How does Jesus describe his return?

Matt. 24:30–31

He will return in a ball of fire.

Q What does Jesus say about our knowledge of the time for his return?

Matt. 24:36–51

It is not known but yet something that one should look forward too.

E14
A2

Matt. 24:37–39a

Q In the context of the Noah story, who are "taken away" (believers) and who are "left behind" (unbelievers)?

Taken away are the ones that love God and left behind do not.

Matt. 24:39b–42

Q When the Son of Man comes back who will be "taken away" and who will be "left behind"?

The people of faith will be taken and those who do not will be left.

Q Convinced that Christ would return in their lifetime, the Thessalonians were concerned about the fate of their Christian friends who had already died. In answer to this, Paul wrote 1 Thessalonians 4:13–18. What does he say about those who have died and those who will still be alive when Jesus returns?

They will all rise whether dead or not just the same.

1 Thess. 4:16

Q How will the Lord return?

He will return in triumph and will take his people home.

Q In 2 Thessalonians 2:1–12, what does Paul say about the Man of Lawlessness regarding when he'll come and what he'll do?

He says that the man will not be taken like others.

Q In Revelation 20, what will happen to Satan during and right after the millennium?

He will lose the power of temptation and dwell with those left behind.

Rev. 20:4–5

Q Who will reign with Christ during the millennium?

He will be the dominant figure to rule over his kingdom.

Q   Who will be thrown into the lake of burning sulfur, and when?   Rev. 20:7–10

Faithfulness and after the coming.

Q   When will the white throne judgment occur?   Rev. 20:11–13

Right before the Lord Comes

Q   Who will be thrown into the lake of fire?   Rev. 20:14–15

Those were not part of the salvation.

Q   Where will the dwelling of God be after the judgment?   Rev. 21:1–4

Gods kingdom

Q   How many gates will be in the New Jerusalem?   Rev. 21:12–14

One

Q   How will believers see God in the New Jerusalem?   Rev. 22:4–5

They will see him as king over all

Q   How long, wide, and high were the New Jerusalem? And how many cubits were its walls?   Rev. 21:15–18

There will be Infinte Amounts of all things.

Q   How will the New Jerusalem be illuminated, and what holds the lamp for that light?   Rev. 21:22–23

The illumination will come from those who believe.

E14
A2

Rev. 22:1–2

Q   How many crops of fruit will be on the tree of life, and how
     many times a year will it bear these crops?

All year long with as many crops
as it sees fit.

Rev. 22:14

Q   Who has the right to the tree of life and to go through the gates
     into the city?

The people who are faithful to God.

Step 2: Find the Meaning of the Story

cf. *TGS*, pp. 394–95

Q   Postmillennialism has recently been gaining new inter-
     est in some Christian camps. Why is it considered an
     optimistic view?

It gives hope that the suffering
will soon be over.

Q   The 1896 hymn "We've a Story to Tell to the Nations" is a
     postmillennial hymn. How does postmillennialism relate
     to evangelism?

It says that both are spreading
some word.

Q   Reading Revelation 20–22 from a postmillennial point of view,
     when is Christ returning?

After the current 1,000 years

cf. *TGS*, pp. 395–96

Q   If you grew up in a church that was not strongly interested in
     end-time issues, you likely grew up as an amillennialist. Amil-
     lennialists reject the idea that the millennium is a period clear-
     ly distinct from the present. What is the argument for this?

That the period has not yet come
but will soon.

E14
A2

Q When does Christ come back according to amillennialism? cf. *TGS*, pp. 395–96

At the end of the 1000 Years or rapture.

Q When will believers and unbelievers be resurrected according to amillennialism? cf. *TGS*, pp. 395–96

believers at the start and not at the end.

Q What does *pre* stand for in premillennialism? cf. *TGS*, pp. 397–98

before

Q How does historic premillennialism differ from amillennialism? cf. *TGS*, pp. 395–98

It gives little hope for a time that is really near.

Q When does Christ return according to historic premillennialism? cf. *TGS*, pp. 397–98

At the beginning of the 1,000 years

Q Who will be judged at the white throne judgment according to historic premillennialism? Rev. 20:11–15; cf. *TGS*, pp. 397–98

All people on the works that they have done.

Q What does *dispensation* refer to in dispensationalism? cf. *TGS*, pp. 398–400

It removes the hopeful sensation that should come with Christs comming.

Q What is the first time Christ will return according to traditional dispensational premillennialism? cf. *TGS*, pp. 398–400

When those who believe out number those that do not.

cf. *TGS*, pp. 398–400

Q   When will Christ come for the third time according to dispensational premillennialism?

To take the rest of the people that may he loyal to him.

cf. *TGS*, pp. 398–400

Q   What is the purpose of the millennium according to traditional dispensational premillennialism?

To convert those who do not have faithfulness to those that do.

Step 3: Make the Story Your Own

Q   Your view of the end times subtly impacts the way you live your Christian life. Try to explain the relationship between one's view on millennialism and one's effort in discipleship of others (being ready for Jesus' sudden return).

One should always strive to help others, but also be ready for the next coming.

Q   How do your convictions about judgment and the eternal state (heaven or hell) impact your evangelism efforts (for your own sake, be honest)?

I am saved so I have little fret that I will not live with the lord.

Q   If your answer to the preceding question is that they don't have much impact, how would you explain that?

It says that those who are saved are saved no matter what the works of life says.

E14
A2

Q   Revelation 21:1 says that God will renew both his own and our dwelling to make them fit for a new eternal relationship between God and his creation. The text talks about renewal rather than destruction in the end. What does this mean for your understanding of heaven (or the eternal state)?

It will be the most beautiful thing that can house all of Gods people.

Q   If the earth shall not "dissolve like snow," like some popular songs proclaim, what does that mean for your understanding of and responsibility toward the earth as we live on it now?

The earth will be for those who are not willing or faithful to the right things.

Q   How would you explain the connection between Revelation 21–22 and Genesis 1–2?

God created the earth and us in his image and he will do the same when we come to be with him.

Conclusion

Terry G. Carter

We hope you enjoyed this journey through God's wonderful story. Many stories interest us, and some even change us due to the powerful message they present. But only one story offers answers to all of life's key questions. God's story helps us understand our individual stories and gives us the foundation for a worldview that allows us to make sense of the world and life in general. Every human asks key life questions when trying to figure out the world and events both past and present. We ask at least four primary questions: Where are we? Who are we? What's wrong in the world? What's the remedy? Every philosophy and religion offers answers, but God's story gives answers that make the most sense.

We live in a world created by the one, sovereign God. Humans were created by God as special beings possessing the image of God and a living soul, allowing us to relate to our creator personally. However, a crisis occurred. God allowed humans to make choices and we chose to rebel, allowing sin to enter creation and pervert all things. Consequently, we live in a world filled with sin and its destructive, deadly power. Yet God loved his creation and provided a solution to the sin problem through his Son, Jesus. Jesus came to earth, taught us a wonderful way of life, and then gave himself as the sacrifice to conquer sin for all humankind. All who believe in him gain eternal life and sin no longer has control.

But it is not enough to know the story and understand its significance. The story must transform life and action. People who accept God's redemptive story of Jesus Christ as the solution to all of sin's deadly power exchange the old life controlled by sin for a new life under the lordship of Christ. People who engage and accept the story "put on Christ." This transformation provides a new worldview and allows believers to see the world and its difficulties in a new way. God's story offers hope, joy, and peace.

James describes the best response to God's story in his letter. "Do not merely listen to the word, and so deceive yourselves. Do what it says" (James 1:22). Let God's story transform your life, your way of thinking, and your very being. Read it, believe it, accept it, and live it. May God bless you in your quest for spiritual truth.